RADIO FREQUENCY IDENTIFICATION HANDBOOK FOR LIBRARIANS

Connie K. Haley, Lynne A. Jacobsen, and Shai Robkin

LIBRARIES
UNLIMITED
A Member of the Greenwood Publishing Group

Westport, Connecticut • London

Library of Congress Cataloging-in-Publication Data

Haley, Connie K.
   Radio frequency identification handbook for librarians / Connie K. Haley,
Lynne A. Jacobsen, and Shai Robkin.
         p. cm.
   Includes bibliographical references and index.
   ISBN-13: 978-1-59158-371-4 (alk. paper)
   ISBN-10: 1-59158-371-3 (alk. paper)
   1. Libraries–Inventory control. 2. Radio frequency identification systems.
I. Jacobsen, Lynne A. II. Robkin, Shai. III. Title.
Z699.7H35 2007
025.00285–dc22   2006032396

British Library Cataloguing in Publication Data is available.

Library of Congress Catalog Card Number: 2006032396
ISBN: 978–1–59158–371–4

First published in 2007

Libraries Unlimited, 88 Post Road West, Westport, CT 06881
A Member of the Greenwood Publishing Group, Inc.
www.lu.com

Printed in the United States of America

The paper used in this book complies with the
Permanent Paper Standard issued by the National
Information Standards Organization (Z39.48–1984).

10   9   8   7   6   5   4   3   2   1

Contents

Acknowledgments

Connie would like to thank her husband, Patrick, and her son, Robert, for their support and editing. She would also like to thank Dean McCrank, Leif Andresen, Bibliotheca, ITG, Libramation, St. LogiTrack, and Tech Logic for their resources and assistance. And finally, Connie would like to thank Sue Easun, Sue Stewart, and Kim Hoag for their help and advice.

Shai would like to thank his wife, Judy, for her many hours of tireless reading, editing, and support. He would also like to thank his staff at ITG for their assistance in this effort. And finally, Shai would like to recognize all the librarians out there who are dealing with or thinking about RFID implementation in their libraries.

Chapter 1

Introduction to RFID

The RFID Handbook for Librarians is the cooperative effort of three individuals who have worked closely with RFID—two librarians, one public and one academic, who have implemented the technology in their libraries, and the vendor who supplied their RFID systems. It is written primarily for professional librarians who are considering RFID and who are trying to decide what system to purchase and which components to include. In addition, those who have already embarked upon this technology path and are seeking to get the most out of their investment will find this book invaluable. It is not a physics book; those seeking to gain a thorough scientific understanding of the technology are advised to consult their nearest science librarian for the best sources written from an engineering perspective. We attempt to explain the basic underpinnings of the technology to the extent necessary to understand how it works in a library environment and how that environment may differ from the other places where RFID is being used.

1.1   WHAT IS RFID?

Radio Frequency Identification is often referred to by the acronym RFID. Most refer to this acronym by sounding out each letter (R-F-I-D). Others sound out the first letter and combine the last three into a single syllable (R-FID). No matter how you write it or say it, you are likely to see more and more of RFID technology playing a role in virtually all walks of life. Although the technology appears to be quite recent, in fact, RFID in different forms has been around for well over a century. RFID tagging of specific items can be traced back to World War II when the British used the system in order to rapidly discriminate between their own returning aircraft and the squadrons of the German Luftwaffe. It was not until the 1980s that RFID applications began to appear in commercial applications, such as railroad freight car tagging, the tagging of cattle and rare dog breeds, automobile immobilizers, keyless entry systems, and automatic highway toll collection. RFID is also being used to track people, from marathon runners to children in amusement parks. With the improved technology, there has been a reduction in cost and size, and RFID has gained wide acceptance in manufacturing and warehouse management. More recently, we have seen widely circulated media reports about the use of RFID by the U.S. Department of Defense (DOD) and large retailers, such as Target and Walmart. But when it comes to individual item-level tagging, libraries find themselves on the cutting edge of this technology. While RFID in a library differs significantly from RFID in other applications, in many ways, librarians are carving out a path that other industries will tread in the future.

Many librarians are familiar with what might be called traditional radio frequency (RF) technology, which has been used for decades for materials security or Electronic Article Surveillance (EAS). Square tags, usually 2-inch square and usually placed under book pockets, set off an alarm at exit gates unless they have been blocked by a metal or metal-impregnated material that effectively detunes (deactivates) the signal. For our purposes here, it is important only to understand that all traditional RF tags are identical and provide no means with which to individually identify any one item. Appending the word "identification" to the words "radio frequency" creates an entirely different world of technology and, most critically, benefits.

The benefits result from the following characteristics of RFID technology:

- Tags can be uniquely encoded with different types of data. Depending on the specific system, much of that data may be changed or rewritten over and over again.
- RFID tags do not require line of sight in order to be read. They can even be read while in motion. In fact, RFID waves can pass through any non-etallic material, including wood and plastic.
- More than one tag can be read at a time.
- Material identification and security can be combined into a single tag.

1.2   HOW DOES THE TAG WORK?

A tag is a simple two-way radio. It receives an RF wave from an antenna attached to an RFID reader, processes the signal, and sends the RFID wave with data stored on the tag back through the antenna to the reader. The reader decodes the signal and sends the tag's information to the computer where a software application that receives the data resides. The reader, which is at the center of this entire process, transmits and receives analog waves and turns them into digital information consisting of strings of ones and zeros. Like all radio signals, the waves emitted by an RFID reader are restricted to specific and limited areas, often called interrogation zones. Only tags within the zone are read.

While there are a number of factors that distinguish tags, all have two basic elements: a computer chip and an antenna. The chip stores information and holds the logic that is necessary to know what to do when it is interrogated. The antenna enables the chip to receive power and communicate with the reader.

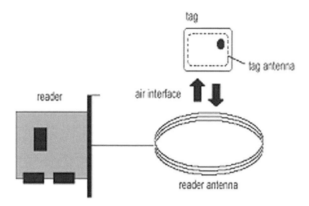

Figure 1.1. A typical transmission sequence consists of a system handshake, data modulation, and data encoding.

1.3 ACTIVE VERSUS PASSIVE TAGS

RFID tags can be active, passive, or semi-passive. While only passive tags are used in library applications, people are most familiar with active tags since they are used for highway toll collection. Active tags have built-in batteries that provide the power that is necessary to run the microchip's circuitry and communicate with the reader. This power source enables the tag to broadcast at great ranges; the most powerful of which can communicate at distances of a half mile or more. However, most are designed to work at ranges that are less than 50 feet. At highway tollbooths, vehicles that have RFID tags mounted to their windshields or dashboards can pass through stations without even slowing down. The battery required to provide this performance is about the size of a pack of playing cards. This size, along with cost and the simple fact that library applications require only relatively limited reading zones, makes active tags impractical for use in libraries.

Passive tags have no power source of their own. Instead, they receive power from the electromagnetic field emitted from the RFID reader. Unlike active tags that can constantly broadcast signals regardless of their proximity to an RFID reader, passive tags remain inactive until they are "woken up" by virtue of their entrance into a reader's interrogation zone. Once a tag is energized, it can send the data contained in the chip's memory back to the reader. Because passive tags rely on external power, they can transmit only over limited distances; depending on the frequency, read ranges are measured in inches.

Figure 1.2. Illinois IPASS.

A limited read range turns out to be ideal for library operations, where numerous RFID-tagged materials are found in close proximity to one another. Additionally, passive tags are small enough to be attached to just about any type of media found in a library.

Semipassive tags use a battery to run the chip's circuitry but communicate by drawing power from the reader's radio waves. They have greater transmission ranges but are larger and more expensive than passive tags (Sweeney, 2005).

1.4 FREQUENCY

All radio communications take place within certain frequencies. Frequency is a measure of how many times an electromagnetic wave goes from one crest to the next in a unit of time as it moves through space. This movement from crest to crest is called a cycle. Frequency is measured in Hertz (Hz), which tells you how many cycles per second occur in an electromagnetic wave (Sweeney, 2005). Passive RFID applications operate in three frequency ranges: low frequency (LF), high frequency (HF), and ultra-high frequency (UHF).

Low frequency operates between 125 and 134 kHz and reads at a very close range, just beyond actual contact. Read ranges are measured in millimeters. LF RFID is frequently used for access control; an employee may place his RFID badge up against a reader to unlock a door or open a gate.

RFID has also been integrated into payment technologies and is widely used by the banking industry in Europe. It is not usually used for the tagging of objects.

High frequency operates at the single frequency of 13.56 MHz. Read ranges are measured in inches, with most standard read applications limited to 6 to 12 inches and EAS applications limited to 36 to 40 inches. Its interrogation field, like LF, is limited in distance. High Frequency is ideal for reading multiple items in close proximity or, as it is commonly referred to in RFID terminology, in near field communication. The HF mode is commonly used for reading tags on drug vials in a pharmacy or books in a library; HF is perfect for item-level tracking. In fact, some RFID tag and equipment manufacturers that specialize in item-level tracking have identified the pharmaceutical and library industries as their prime growth markets. Librarians may not often be able to claim that they are at the forefront of technological innovation, but in the case of item level RFID, such a claim is definitely justified.

Ultra-high frequency operates at ranges between 868 and 954 MHz. The available ranges vary from country to country. In the United States, that range is restricted to 902 to 928 MHz. Read ranges are measured in feet; in perfect environments, UHF works at 30 to 40 feet or more. However, most applications do not require a read range greater than that of a typical warehouse loading dock door, 10 to 12 feet. Unlike the contained fields of LF and HF systems, UHF emits a "propagating" electric field that is easily reflected. The buzz heard recently about RFID revolves around UHF applications for supply chains and asset management. Much talk revolves around large retailers, such as Walmart and Target, who have begun to mandate that their vendors tag pallets and cases with UHF RFID tags.

The standards created for UHF are separate from those that have been adopted for HF; standards for HF are limited to what are generally referred to as technology standards, how readers and tags communicate with each other. These standards include ISO 14443 for ticketing, ISO 15693 for access control, and ISO 18000 for item tracking. Note that the HF standards do not address specific applications. On the other hand, the world of UHF includes a number of application standards, including Automotive Industry Action Group (AIAG) for the automotive industry, UPU for the postal system, International Air Transport Association (IATA) for airlines, Global Tag (GTAG^{TM}) for supply chain (GTAG^{TM} is a standardization initiative of the European Article Number Association and the Uniform Code Council EAN/UCC), and most importantly Electronic Product Code (EPC). EPC is the RFID equivalent of the Universal Product Code (UPC) found in bar codes. We will discuss EPC at greater length in our discussion of RFID in retail below.

1.5   RFID IN RETAIL

At the current time, retailers are not tagging individual products and it is likely to be several years before they do, if they do at all. Should item-level tagging be used in retail, it will be based on the same 13.56 MHz HF RFID that is used in libraries and the pharmaceutical industry. Many people speculate about the potential effect that widespread use of RFID in retail would have on libraries. The prime focus is on the bottom line, the cost of tags. The enormous volume of tags required to tag every item in Wal-Mart alone promises to drive down tag prices for libraries as well. While the emergence of item-level tagging in retail would affect other industries, there are good reasons to believe that the effect on libraries will be limited. An understanding of the differences between retail and library environments from an RFID perspective makes this clear.

First and foremost, libraries require re-usable asset-tracking technology as opposed to the disposable asset-tracking technology that is sufficient for retail.

Libraries require tags that will last for years, if not decades; in most instances, the lifespan of a tag placed on a product for sale need not be greater than a few months. Tags used in libraries must be able to withstand potentially thousands of read/write cycles. Retail tags are likely to be read only once at each station along the supply chain that starts in the manufacturing plant and ends at the cash register of the neighborhood retailer. Every effort continues to be made to drive down the cost of retail tags; every possible corner will be cut within the particular constraints of specific product categories in order to drive prices lower. We are likely to see a variety of tags designed to meet different supply-chain parameters. The same tag is not likely to be used on both a baseball bat and a bouquet of fresh flowers. If a product's lifespan from point of production to sale is likely to be a week and if savings can be achieved by manufacturing tags that only last a week, it makes no sense to use a tag that survives any longer. In the case of libraries, however, we are often talking decades.

Libraries fall into the category of a "closed loop market" as opposed to retail, which falls into the "open chain market" category. Library materials move in and out of the same library or library system over and over. Unless it is returned, a retail product is unlikely to land in the same place more than once. More importantly, open chain markets are open to potentially anyone and everyone. Millions of razor blades may be manufactured in a single plant and they are just as likely to end up on the shelves of Walmart as they would on the shelves of the corner drugstore. As a result, open chain markets cannot rely on a common database to be a repository of information to which all parties in the supply chain refer; the tag itself must hold all the data that may be needed.

On the other hand, an individual library or library system is self-contained. As such, tags need contain only the amount of information necessary to link a specific item to its record in the database. This allows libraries a great degree of individual flexibility in their choice of applications as well as the option to customize applications for their particular needs.

The single characteristic that distinguishes open and closed systems is the item identifier or numbering scheme. Open systems require a strictly regulated system of identification to ensure that there is no duplication and that all databases conform to a consistent data structure. This is accomplished through the EPC. Just like with UPC, manufacturers are assigned specific number ranges that may be used to identify their individual products. And each product must be assigned a unique number. The EPC specifications include data length, structure, and position. Shown below is a typical EPC. The header tells the RFID reader what type of number follows, whether it is a standard EPC or some variant. The EPC manager number identifies the company or manufacturer. The object class is a stock-keeping unit (SKU). The EPC manager number and object class taken together identify the specific product, such as a 16-ounce box of Cheerios. The serial number identifies the specific 16-ounce box of Cheerios.

When a tag is manufactured, it is uniquely identified with an individual serial number, EPC, or some other number. However, this number is not used by libraries in their operations and, in fact, for all intents and purposes, the number need not exist. Libraries assign RFID numbers using the same scheme that they use for bar codes. As we will see in our discussion of tagging, during the initial conversion to RFID, most systems require only that the existing bar code be scanned in order to program the RFID tag. The barcode number assignment is random; whatever number comes next off the sheet or roll of bar codes is used. Care must be taken, of course, to ensure that the item is uniquely identified. There is no guarantee that an item belonging to one library system will not be duplicated by a different library system. However, because libraries are closed loop systems, it is unlikely that a book from one library, having the same bar-code number as a book in another library, will ever be taken to the first library.

In theory, EPCs could be used as identifiers of library materials. However, it would be impractical to do so for a number of reasons. It is highly unlikely that libraries would be prepared to drop their well-established numbering systems that have functioned effectively and efficiently for years. The random assignment of numbers to materials serves the interest of patron privacy well. Without access to the library's database, the bar-code number is meaningless. On the other hand, EPCs, just like UPCs and ISBNs, identify items to anyone with access to the EPC database; in order to be useful, the database must be available to everyone along the supply chain. We address privacy concerns as they relate to RFID in more detail in Chapter 2.

With an understanding of how RFID in libraries differs from RFID in other industries, we can turn our attention to the specifics of the technology within a library environment. As we have shown here, all library RFID systems, regardless of the tag and reader manufacturer or the integration vendor, use 13.56-MHz passive HF tags that must withstand thousands (if not tens of thousands) of read/write cycles. That said, we shall see that there are a number of different ways to skin the library RFID cat.

REFERENCE

Sweeney, P. J., II. (2005). *RFID for dummies: A reference for the rest of us.* Indianapolis, IN: Wiley Publishing.

Chapter 2

Considering Implementation of RFID

This chapter addresses the advantages and concerns of implementing RFID technology in your library, in addition to the discussion of RFID data structure, and important issues. In this chapter, the terms check in and check out are used interchangeably with charge and discharge.

Radio Frequency Identification (RFID) has the potential to speed up library services and streamline time-consuming operations, such as check in, sorting, and inventory. Librarians considering implementation of RFID must be aware that the RFID industry is rapidly evolving. Frequently, new companies are being formed while older companies are being acquired by other companies. New products are emerging and protocols are changing (Sweeney, 2005).

Despite all the improvements made within the industry in recent years, RFID technology still has its limitations, such as radio-wave interference, privacy implications, and so on. It is important to recognize these shortcomings and how they affect the decision to implement. As library community interest in RFID has grown, so have concerns about its implications on privacy, health standards, standardization, and interoperability. Additionally, librarians want assurance that their substantial investment will deliver anticipated returns—better services for patrons, tighter security and theft protection for materials, better inventory control and collection management, and more efficient and effective use of library staff.

RFID expert Lichtenberg (2005) listed the advantages, such as widely available, relatively inexpensive, better inventory control, increased self check; and disadvantages, such as high start-up costs, indirect return on investment, immaturity of middleware, lower than expected accuracy, and immature standards. Lichtenberg said that libraries considering implementation need to focus on supporting their patrons and understanding their needs better. Normally we think of RFID dataflow in libraries in only one direction, from the tag to the reader to the middleware to the library systems. The reverse flow of information will actually provide more important information (Lichtenberg, 2005). Lichtenberg's comments remind me of Lawrence McCrank's presentation at the ALA 2005 RFID program (McCrank, 2005). McCrank called for intelligent and creative applications for library RFID to better serve user needs, such as the possibilities of integrating course management software and eReserves software into the RFID. RFID technology has many advantages. In the next section we will discuss the advantages of using RFID in libraries.

2.1   ADVANTAGES OF USING RFID

In Chapter 1, we emphasized that libraries are on the cutting edge of item-level RFID technology. While it is exciting to be an innovator and a technological leader, it is important that libraries considering RFID stay focused on the ultimate benefits that they seek to achieve. There may be many ways to improve library operations; RFID may not be the best solution for every objective. We should think of RFID the same way that we would think of a photocopier. We purchase a photocopier in order to make copies, not to have a sophisticated piece of equipment sitting in the corner of our office. If some means other than a photocopier is faster, easier, or less expensive, that solution will win the day. For example, previously, many documents that might have been copied are now scanned into a computer. That is why the Xerox Corporation has redefined itself as a document management company and not a copier company.

Similarly, libraries are most likely to make the right decision concerning RFID by focusing on ultimate benefits—lower costs, better service, and improved work environments. We will examine the potential benefits of RFID from the perspectives of its three stakeholders—the library as an organization, its staff, and its patrons.

2.1.1   Benefits to Library Staff

Library circulation staff get the most benefits from RFID technology, such as reducing the repetitive stress injuries, reducing time needed for circulation operations, and so on. Acquisition staff may benefit from RFID in the near future.

Reducing the repetitive stress injuries.

RFID technology can automatically identify an item without requiring line of sight, which reduces staff time in operations and reduces the costs associated with staff time. This allows the circulation staff to reduce the repetitive stress injuries, such as carpal tunnel syndrome during check out, check in, and sort processes. It is not difficult to measure the labor savings achieved by reducing or altogether eliminating staff involvement in materials handling processes. The costs that might be incurred in the absence of RFID or other labor-saving technologies, most importantly those associated with repetitive stress injuries such as carpal tunnel syndrome, are more difficult to measure. Given the litigious nature of American society, it is not surprising that libraries have seen workman's compensation claims and insurance rates jump in recent years.

Less time needed for circulation operations.

RFID technology reduces the amount of time required to perform circulation operations. It can charge or discharge several items at the same time (vs. bar code that can check out only one item at a time) at staff circulation workstations. Library materials stacked up to 6 inches high or six items may be checked out all at the same time. No separate process is required for deactivating or reactivating the security component. Radio Frequency Identification can help to remove staff altogether from routine circulation processes.

Automated check in can further reduce staff time required for materials handling. While patron self check-in has been available to libraries using traditional bar-code technology for a number of years, equipment costs and user complexity have severely limited its adoption. On the other hand, relatively inexpensive standard book drops can be retrofitted with RFID readers so that items passing through return chutes are immediately checked in and their security component reactivated. Patrons continue to return materials, as they always have, simply by dropping them into slots.

RFID can also expedite the sorting process needed to direct materials to their proper location after they have been returned. Tags can be programmed to store location information, or this data can be extracted from the ILS. If the library is using automated material handling (AMH, the ability to automatically sort and move materials on a conveyor), the location information is used to move materials into their proper bins without staff intervention. This process relieves circulation staff from excessive grasping and handling of items for scanning, sensitizing and desensitizing, and sorting (San Francisco Public Library Technology and Privacy Advisory Committee, 2005). RFID tags can also be used to identify library and branch information for libraries that allow inter-library and intra-library borrowing. Hold items and other exceptions can be separated into different bins, further reducing staff handling time. All this can be done at a fraction of the cost required for a bar-code-based AMH system.

2.1.2   Benefits to Libraries

All organizations, not for profits as well as for profits, when operating rationally, seek to maximize their deliverables at the lowest possible cost. RFID, properly implemented in the right places, has the potential of doing just that for libraries.

Security.

One benefit to libraries is a potentially better security. Some vendors' tags have a built-in security bit (Shigo, 2003), Electronic Article Surveillance (EAS). Most RFID systems include EAS functionality, thereby eliminating the need to attach an additional security strip to an item. The security bit in the tag is a unique powerful bursting bit that is unlike any other bit in the tag. It is this bursting bit that the security gates detect. Some RFID security systems are server based, and others are server database independent (see Security section later in this chapter for more information). Currently, the security bit detection performance exceeds that of the RFID security system that relies on a server-based database, even though Application Family Identifier (AFI) may be a standardized security functionality in the future (see Data Model section in this chapter for more information). By combining library item identification and security into one tag, libraries minimize labeling time and its associated cost. As noted previously, libraries have the option of printing sequential bar-code numbers on the RFID overlay labels for new items, so there is no need to affix an additional bar-code label. The authors believe that utilization of RFID tags with AFI for security could be the direction that RFID technology might take. Libraries should consider this feature when choosing an RFID vendor.

RFID security technology is subject to fewer false alarms than traditional radio frequency (RF) and electromagnetic (EM) technology. Depending on the specific system, RFID security detection rates, commonly referred to as "pick rates," can be superior to other forms of detection, especially for print, and to a somewhat lesser degree for magnetic media. Among the items that present some problems for RFID are CDs and DVDs (as discussed in the section below dealing with RFID concerns and considerations). As previously noted, security is automatically deactivated and reactivated as materials are checked out and in; no separate security procedures are required. The RFID exit gates can not only alert staff to the unauthorized removal of an item, but also record that item's identification. Libraries using traditional EM security technology regularly report that due to the prevalence of false alarms and a natural aversion to confrontation, staff regularly wave patrons through after the exit alarm goes off. Staff persons are more inclined to "confront" patrons when they know that the security alarm went off for a good reason and when they can ask to see a specific item. Specific item information can also be used in overall collection management. Though RFID security gates have many advantages, they are not perfect. More discussions are included in the last section of this chapter.

Inventory.

RFID technology can also reduce the costs associated with taking library inventory. From a shelf-reading perspective, the leap from bar codes to RFID is even greater than was the move from manual data collection to bar codes. Even once their entire collections were bar coded, many libraries considered inventory taking such an onerous task that they never even attempted it. An RFID reader scans items on the shelves at rates that, depending on the system used, are five, or even twenty times faster than with barcode reading. Books need not be tipped or pulled from shelves; they do not, in fact, need to be touched at all. In addition to being fast, shelf reading using RFID technology is also much less physically taxing on the operator.

Stacks management.

The inventory process can also identify items that are out of proper order. RFID technology can also be used to manage materials on the shelves—to find items that are missing and to identify items that have been misshelved. Some RFID systems enhance materials security with shelf-reading applications that ensure that all security bits are activated at the same time that inventory is taken. All these functions—inventory, item search, shelf order, and even security activation, if available—can be done at the same time. An added benefit is that when not being used for shelf reading, libraries can use hand-held devices to track reference-material usage by scanning books before reshelving.

2.1.3   Benefits to Patrons

As previously noted, RFID technology not only reduces the amount of time required for staff to perform circulation operations, but also provides better self-service capabilities. One way or the other, patrons spend less time waiting in check-out lines. In addition, technologically advanced services enhance the average patron's attitude toward the library, particularly with taking advantage of self-service capabilities. Citizens who pump their own gas, check out their own groceries and hardware purchases, and check themselves in at the airport have come to expect the same type of technological sophistication in libraries. Not only does self service reduce check-out wait times by removing staff involvement, but it also enhances patron privacy.

Patron self check.

At self check-out workstations, patrons can check out library materials stacked up to 6 inches high or six items all at the same time. Patrons need not hunt for bar codes or confuse the library label with the ISBN. Like staff, they can place everything that they want to check out on readers, all at the same time, without regard to orientation. Because RFID waves do not damage magnetically stored media, no special process is needed for the handling of video or audio cassettes.

Automated check in provides patrons with real time credit to their accounts. They can immediately check out additional materials without exceeding the library established limit and at the same time reduce or eliminate late fines. Some libraries also provide patrons a returns receipt option. A sorting system's ability to separate materials on reserve upon receipt of the items means that patrons get their reserve requests without waiting additional days to receive them. Improved collection and shelf management ensure that materials that should be in the library are actually there. Improved shelf organization means that patrons find what they are looking for quickly and easily.

Patrons, as well as staff, also appreciate the fact that bar-code labels no longer need to be placed on the outside of book covers, often obscuring text or graphics. Where library system or consortium conformance does not preclude it, bar codes should be printed on or placed over the RFID tags that are affixed to the inside of the back covers.

Improved patron services.

Experience has shown that RFID technology can improve patron services even when libraries are facing staff shortages and budget cuts due to decreased funding from both state government and local government. Jackie Griffin, director of the Berkeley Public Library, stated that the library had capital funding to double the size of their building but they had no corresponding increase in operating budget. In order to serve more people with the same number of staff they needed to turn to technological solution, RFID. As a result of labor savings by using RFID technology, the Berkeley Public Library was able to re-open on Sundays and to return their book purchasing budget to near normal levels (Smart, 2005). Its patrons benefited from the fact that despite budget cuts, they had no loss in services and the number of available publications was not decreased.

Conclusion.

The use of RFID is also superior to bar code in some important ways. Bar codes can be affected by rain, dirt, and dust, while RFID tags are not subject to these problems. Staff members do not have to reprint and reaffix RFID tags as they would in the case of bar codes. In addition, the RFID streamlines workflow in the area of self service, books return, shelf management, and inventory. However, the RFID technology has its potential disadvantages in libraries.

2.2   RFID CONCERNS

As with every major change that a library undertakes, there are serious concerns and considerations that must be carefully examined. They fall into five categories: political/social, economic, technical, physical, and organizational. Many librarians perceive concerns as challenges to be overcome. Therefore we point out the RFID concerns, and try to find the best solutions for these challenges as well.

2.2.1   Political/Social Concerns

Privacy.

The perceived threats to privacy are the major concern of RFID in libraries. Of all the concerns and issues with RFID implementation in libraries, privacy tops the list. Privacy advocates worry about unauthorized tag reading. For example, a stranger, or a hacker, on the street can use RFID readers to discover the book titles and personal information on the RFID patron cards. Authors would suggest that to address the concerns of privacy advocates, libraries should be careful to include only the minimum amount of information on the tag (for more information see Data Structure discussed later in this chapter). A bar-code number on a library item tag is useless for a stranger, or a hacker, on the street as long as the bar code is not searchable on the library's online catalog. Similarly an institution number on a patron card is no use for a stranger, or a hacker, unless he/she has access to the secured institution computer systems. ALA recommends that a library let users be aware of the RFID technology in the library, and label all RFID equipment (American Library Association, 2005).

The use of RFID technology has engendered considerable controversy because some people are concerned that the tag on the book could be used to identify items that an individual has borrowed from the library even if they are packed away in a backpack, book bag, or pocketbook. There are those who also believe that the use of RFID can in someway compromise a patron's private library record. And some people have gotten the impression that RFID can be used to track a person's movements.

A typical scenario for concern is described as follows. A person with the necessary technical skills and access to an appropriate RFID reader could stand outside the library (or anywhere else for that matter) and read the titles of whatever items Mr. Library Patron had put away in his briefcase. To make things even worse, he could read the personal information stored on Mr. Patron's RFID library card. Finally, should he desire to follow Mr. Patron, he could track his movements without having to get closer than a half mile.

Let us address these concerns in reverse order. First, as we pointed out in Chapter 1, the passive HF (high frequency) RFID tags used in libraries have a limited read range, usually only about 6 inches. RFID and GPS (Global Positioning System) technologies are totally different. Library RFID system involves no satellites. Second, most libraries, if for no other reason than cost, choose not to use RFID patron cards. However, should RFID patron cards be used, the information on them contains a randomly assigned number which is meaningless without access to the library's database. Finally, if there is one thing that all libraries can agree upon concerning RFID standards, it is that no bibliographic information should be stored on tags. Should Mr. Snoop get close enough to Mr. Patron to read what is in his briefcase, all that would be revealed would be a randomly assigned number. Just like patron numbers, item numbers are meaningless without a lookup in the database. Libraries can choose to store item status, branch ownership, part number, or even shelving location on tags. Under no circumstances should bibliographic information be kept on the tag. As we explain in Chapter 3, there is nothing to be gained by doing so.

Some privacy advocates have pointed out that these random numbers can be made meaningful through reverse lookup. Mr. Snoop first collects a list of all the titles and their associated bar-code numbers on a specific subject, such as bomb making. He can then compare the bar-code numbers extracted from RFID tags with those on the list to determine titles. While this is, in the authors' opinion, a rather far-fetched proposition, we recommend that an additional privacy precaution be taken by not including bar-code numbers as a searchable parameter in the library's online catalog.

Some have suggested encryption in response to hard-line privacy advocates. While encryption may serve to mollify some, it is not likely to satisfy all. Moreover, encryption comes with a number of costs, most importantly interoperability. The ALA is well respected throughout North America as a guardian of privacy and personal freedom. Hopefully, a firm written statement from the library's RFID vendor, stating that it adheres to the guidelines set out by ALA concerning privacy, will be sufficient to calm the fears of the vast majority of the community.

Health.

After reviewing studies and reports issued by the World Health Organization (WHO), California Department of Health Services (CDHS), National Council on Radiation Protection and Measurement (NCRP), a part of the UK Health Protection Agency, National Institute of Occupational Safety and Health (NIOSH), Federal Communication Commission (FCC), the National Institute of Environmental Health Sciences (NIEHS), and International Commission on Non Ionizing Radiation Protection (ICNIRP), the San Francisco Public Library Technology and Privacy Advisory Committee (2005) drew the following conclusions:

Currently available research and studies on radio frequency exposure to devices in the 10 MHz to 300 GHz frequency range do not suggest any health risks from RF exposures below guideline levels. The biological evidence does not suggest causal association between exposures to RF fields and the risk of cancer.

Further research is needed to address uncertainties in current RFID knowledge; Manufacturers of medical devices and security systems should provide sufficient information about current and new products to minimize risk of emissions from security systems interfering with electrically powered active medical devices, such as pacemakers. (p. 26–27)

Community education.

When putting new systems in place, it is important to proactively communicate with library patrons to alleviate concerns and fears. One of the stumbling blocks to patron acceptance of RFID is the lack of knowledge about what RFID is used for, what effect it has on patrons, and why it is necessary. Patrons should be educated on how the library is using RFID and what benefits the patrons can expect to get from its use. Librarians have been doing an excellent job of raising awareness of RFID issues. And they have strong concerns about the rights of patrons and the need to protect their privacy and health. Clearly and simply stated information on security and safety should be shared with patrons. Raising patron awareness will help the libraries gain acceptance of the technology, increasing the odds for a successful conversion.

Staff buy-in.

Labor-saving technologies inevitably put a scare into the workplace. Some employees are concerned that they will lose their jobs while others fear that they are not sufficiently computer literate to operate the new system. Additionally, there are always a few people that resist change, regardless of its nature. If a library has too many staff persons that fall into this last category, it may need to abandon the entire RFID idea.

Library administrators are wise to educate and involve staff throughout the entire process, from deciding whether to investigate the technology or not, to choosing a vendor and implementation. Soliciting staff input and suggestions is the best way to ensure staff buy-in. Directors must emphasize that the objective of RFID implementation is to allow staff to engage in more productive and more interesting duties (like assisting patrons). They should explain that labor savings will come through attrition, not through firing. Most importantly, it must be made clear that RFID benefits not only patrons and the library as an institution, but staff as well.

Benefits.

Though the RFID provides convenience for users to check out library materials via self services, generally speaking, the benefits for library users are less than the benefits for the library staff, especially for circulation services staff.

2.2.2 Economic Concerns

Tags.

The price of an RFID tag is significantly higher than that of bar-code labels ($.02 to $.03) /EM strip combinations. The price of a security strip ranges from $.125 to $.15 per book and approximately $1 per CD/DVD. The total security cost for one book is about $.145 to $.18. The tag is priced between $.50 and $.70 each from library RFID vendors in 2005. One CD/DVD tag is about $1.45 (San Francisco Public Library Technology and Privacy Advisory Committee, 2005). A customized label with a bar code and library logo cost between $.002 and $.10. The total costs of one RFID tag and one label could be much higher than the costs of bar code, ranging from $.52 to $1.55.

In addition to the price of the tags, the library must also consider the labor cost for tagging and conversion from bar code to RFID. The most expensive aspects of RFID technology in libraries are the cost of the tag, the cost of labor of placing the tag on each item, and converting the bar-code number onto the tag (Ayre, 2004). As we shall see in Chapter 3, RFID tag programming is a relatively simple process. The conversion process consists of placing the tag on each item and converting the bar code onto the tag. However, the conversion of an entire collection requires significant labor resources. The process is labor intensive. Library administrators may consider using volunteers to minimize the cost of the conversion project. Some libraries, including the Chicago State University Library and the Warren-Newport Public Library, have used volunteers extensively to both cut conversion costs and get the job done more quickly. For cost-saving techniques, please see Chapter 5. Anyway, the cost in labor and time must be factored into the initial conversion costs.

Analysts from independent research companies Gartner and Forrester Research agreed that a tag price less than $0.10 (production volume of one billion units) is achievable in 6 to 8 years, thus limiting near term prospects for widespread adoption of passive RFID. The high demand for the tags from Wal-Mart, Department of Defense (DOD), etc., has created a big enough market to support these prices. Other analysts believe such prices are achievable within 15 years. Many librarians are waiting for the price to come down further before considering RFID technology, while others are waiting to see whether RFID will become cost effective enough to replace bar-coding technology altogether (Mesenbrink, 2002). There is little doubt that tag cost will continue to drop and in all likelihood, prices are lower today than they were when this book was written.

Unfortunately, it is not justified to believe that library RFID tag prices are likely to drop into the single digits as some are predicting for tags used in retail applications. See Chapter 1 for a discussion of the difference between RFID tags in libraries and tags used in other industries.

Equipment and software.

Radio Frequency Identification systems are sold a la carte. All libraries must invest in tags, collection conversion, at least one tag programming unit, and at least one staff circulation station (in some systems, staff stations are capable of doing both programming and circulation). Other components—self check-out, automated returns, sorting, stack maintenance, and security—are optional. The a la carte nature of an RFID system purchase means that implementation need not be done all at once. Libraries must take into account changes in operations when evaluating their equipment needs. For example, RFID implementation should result in a reduction in staff stations, both public and back room.

The wide variety of approaches that RFID vendors have taken toward different library applications makes it almost impossible to include meaningful pricing information on hardware and software. In fact, how hardware and software are sold varies from vendor to vendor. Some sell bundled packages including both, while others sell individual hardware components and software licenses separately. Still others sell system or site licenses for some or all of their software applications, allowing customers to secure hardware components wherever they can find them. What complicates pricing comparisons even further is the fact that some systems require certain hardware and even software components that are not required by others. For example, a staff station from one vendor may consist of only RFID hardware and software, while another will also include all the other components required—computer, monitor, bar-code scanner, and receipt printer. Therefore, it is important, before a library solicits an RFID quote or bid, to have a pretty good idea of how it wants the various components to be broken out.

Support and maintenance.

The ongoing annual expense of hardware and software maintenance and support must also be included in the evaluation. Most vendors include the first year's support and maintenance in the purchase price of the system and are prepared to lock in future coverage for at least 5 more years. Support cost, which are usually quoted as a percentage of component list or purchase price, can be as high as 18%. Therefore, a system that may look affordable based on its initial purchase price may not be sustainable over the course of its anticipated operating life. While the purchase of an RFID system usually comes out of a special capital budget, annual maintenance usually comes out of a library's operating budget.

Additional associated costs.

Most RFID components can be installed in an existing library with little or no changes in infrastructure. Libraries implementing RFID will want, however, to rethink the layout of their buildings to take best advantage of the technology. This may mean more self check-out stations and fewer staff stations or it could include designating one staff station to provide assistance to multiple self check-out stations. Electrical and network wiring is required in most RFID applications. Some applications necessitate the purchase of additional computer equipment. The greatest potential infrastructure cost is likely to be the modifications required to accommodate a sorting system in the building. Often, this type of modification will include changes required to meet fire codes.

Many (and with some systems all) RFID applications require SIP2 or NCIP, the protocol provided by the library's ILS vendor that interfaces the ILS database with third-party products. Libraries anticipating migration to RFID should think ahead and include SIP2 or NCIP when negotiating the purchase or renewal of an ILS contract.

The relatively short period that RFID has now been in use in libraries makes it difficult to determine the ROI (return on investment). While some of the benefits derived from the system are measurable, such as labor savings, others, such as customer satisfaction, are much more difficult to quantify. Hopefully long-term ROI data will become available in the coming years.

2.2.3   Technical Concerns

The Achilles heel of RFID technology is metal, in particular the metal content of CDs and DVDs. The section on tags in Chapter 3 discusses this problem at length. As the technology stands today, RFID is not an effective tool for detecting the theft of disks unless it is combined with some sort of AV locking case system.

Interference.

RFID waves pass through wood, paper, and plastic. However, books with foil covers do not mix well with radio waves. For example, the Chicago State University Library converted its collections of 400,000 volumes to the RFID. Less than 10 books are covered with foil. However, public libraries with larger fiction and paperback collections have many more foil covered books than academic libraries. Libraries with quantities of foil covered books may need to put them in a separate location. The most popular solution, discussed in Chapter 5, is to replace foil covers with paper covers.

Interference may cause a high loss rate in libraries. For example, a thief, using foil to wrap library items, may subvert the RFID security gates. The shielding problem of foil covers points to a fundamental weakness of RFID as a theft-prevention tool. Like traditional radio frequency (RF) tags, RFID tags enveloped in metal, such as a foil lined bag, cannot be detected. In addition, unlike EM strips that are embedded within spines or deep between pages, RFID tags are clearly visible. A preprinted tag or, even better, a tag covered with a printed label, serves to camouflage its purpose. However, a knowledgeable and committed thief will quickly discover how the system works.

Library collections stored on metal shelves and metal bins used for high density storage can interfere with RFID. In most cases, this problem is restricted to items that are next to metal end panels and uprights (the first and last books on a shelf). To be certain that shelf-reading operations are not likely to be significantly impaired, libraries should request that prospective vendors demonstrate their inventory applications on site.

The RFID security gates do not work well with books or AV materials that have tags placed in the same position. Most libraries alternate the tag positions at the back of the book cover. Detailed information is in the section of Tag Placement in Chapter 3. Some CDs and DVDs have metal in the middle circles that interfere with doughnut-shaped RFID tags. A library may choose to place the tag on the AV cases as a solution to this type of interference.

What about the library's existing electromagnetic (EM) or radio frequency (RF) security systems? The RFID security system will not detect EM or RF tags and EM and RF systems will not detect RFID tags. However, RFID tags will not interfere with the tags from the other security systems and the other tags need not interfere with the reading of RFID tags. EM and RF systems can continue to be used throughout the tagging process up until the new RFID gates are installed and the system goes live. The old EM or RF tags may be left in place even after the RFID system is fully operational. It is important to note, however, that RFID tags should not be placed over RF tags or directly opposite them (for example, if the RF tag is on the outside cover near the spine at the same spot that the RFID tag would be placed on the inside of the cover) to avoid the tags' interference. Complexity is another concern besides interference.

Complexity.

RFID is obviously more complex than bar-code technology. A bar-code label can be printed by just about any printer and read by any off-the-shelf scanner that is equipped to read the Code 39 and Codabar symbologies used in libraries. Library staff do not need much special knowledge to use systems that employ bar-code technology. More RFID training is needed for circulation staff and technical services staff to make sure that they are capable of handling RFID. Depending on the applications implemented, an RFID system requires a variety of specialized equipment. More knowledge is needed for system librarians and computer technicians to make sure that they are able to maintain and troubleshoot the RFID system. Library administrators need to acquire adequate knowledge to make the right policies for libraries and the library consortium. Library administrators must educate themselves sufficiently in order to choose the right RFID hardware, software, and vendor. Circulation and technical services staff need special training to ensure that they are capable of maintaining and troubleshooting the RFID system.

Libraries migrating to RFID will not be ditching their bar-code scanners anytime soon. Most will continue to use bar-code-based patron cards for the foreseeable future. Dual support for both RFID and bar-code technology must be maintained for inter-library loans and reciprocal borrowing, especially in consortium environments.

A library that is using RFID needs to continue using bar codes and bar-code equipment for inter-library loans and reciprocal borrowing in consortium environments. A library in a consortium needs to support both bar code and RFID for many years.

Can one library rewrite another library's RFID in a library consortium? Before the first library in the consortia implements RFID technology, a consortia policy and procedure should be discussed and established to eliminate problems of compatibility and interoperability. The consortium policy needs to pay attention to national and international standards, including library RFID data structure (more discussion later in the section of Data Model in this chapter) to achieve interoperability. The consortium RFID policy would make the application of RFID technology most effective for every library in the consortia.

A consortium-recommended vendor is very useful for compatibility. A consortium negotiation of purchasing is powerful and can lower the RFID price for all libraries in the consortium.

In a larger RFID environment, a library book or DVD may set off an alarm at a bookstore or retail store. The Danish RFID Working Group has been working on solutions with other related parties. See Data Model later in this chapter for more information. Besides the complexity of the RFID technology, radio waves' interference is another concern.

Standardization.

Standards process takes a long time while technology grows rapidly. There are gaps between the RFID standards and the RFID products. Tags and equipment from different vendors may not be compatible. Make sure the vendor's products are ISO 18000 compliant and backward compatible when you write the RFP.

The most perplexing technical issue confronting librarians, first in deciding to implement RFID and second in choosing a vendor, is that of standards or, to be more precise, the absence of standards. No one wants to be caught holding Beta when VHS wins the day. Those interested in the details of this matter of standards are encouraged to read the tags section in Chapter 3. We can summarize the conclusions reached there rather quickly. The relevant RFID standards that do exist are technology standards, not application standards. As such, there are no standards at this time that specifically address RFID in North American libraries. Due to the dynamics of the industry, the diversity of North American libraries, and the democratic nature of decision making in this part of the world, a clear application standard for library RFID is not likely to emerge for many years. The ALA (American Library Association), NISO RFID Working Group will continue to discuss and address the issue. Libraries that prefer to wait for such a standard before migrating to RFID are likely to find themselves waiting for a long time.

In order to make common access to tags workable in terms of compatibility and interoperability, a set of policies and procedures for the institutions that share materials must be established up front to eliminate potential problems. The policies should set the standards and data definitions that will be used by all the institutions in the group. Policies that are set should employ available national and international standards, whenever possible, in order to achieve interoperability. An overall policy makes the application of RFID technology across institutions viable. If a single RFID vendor is not selected for all members, a commitment to share information for the purpose of interoperability, from each participating vendor, should be elicited.

Currently, RFID software is tied with a particular RFID vendor. If a library buys tags and RFID hardware from different vendors, the RFID software could be different, even though the tags and hardware are made by the same manufacturer. Baker & Taylor, a bookseller, gave a vivid example (Bitner, 2005). Baker & Taylor has been processing library materials with RFID tags since 2002. Their library customers use a variety of vendors, each of which has supplied Baker & Taylor with its own tags, hardware, and software. It was very difficult for Baker & Taylor to manage tags and terminals. It was also difficult to ensure that the right RFID tags were programmed correctly and applied to the right customer's books. Due to each RFID vendor having its own software, converting barcode numbers to the tag process is different from each vendor. Baker & Taylor discovered great differences between systems in terms of the user friendlessness of conversion software. Some vendors' conversion software is easier to use than others. While Baker & Taylor, like other book processors, has found a way to work with all the existing RFID systems, its experience points out the deficiencies in interoperability at the current time.

Other RFID software required for library applications includes circulation staff station, self check-out station, automatic book drop, sorting with conveyors, inventory, and customized reports. For example, Chicago State University Library requested its vendor to provide customized software reporting built-in with the tag conversion software to monitor the initial conversion project. The report can list the bar codes that were converted to the tag. Hopefully, in the near future, the RFID software could be standardized for tags and hardware from all vendors.

Accuracy.

There are technical problems with tag scanning accuracy. Tags are functioning at success rates of less than 100%. Tag readers are not always reliable. Antennae sometimes become separated from their tags due to the nature of the tag's manufacturing. Other problems occur in trying to read tags through foil book covers, DVD metal circle, and so on. For security reasons, rewritable tags have to be locked after writing. This operation is not reversible. For more information please read the FAQs section in the Appendix.

Withdrawing process.

RFID tags may add more work in the withdrawing process if they have to be removed or cut from materials before being discarded. Peeling off tags from library materials is time-consuming work. Librarians should consider cutting tags in half, which takes less time than peeling tags off materials. On the bright side, RFID tags can be more easily removed than electromagnetic security strips hidden in the spines or between pages of books.

Peeling off tags.

The RFID tag can be more easily removed than an electromagnetic security strip that is hidden down spines or between pages. The solution is to make the tag look like a book plate by using a label to cover the tag with a library logo, bar code, or other visible information. A potential future solution will be that publishers embed the tags in books and other library materials.

2.2.4   Physical Concerns

We noted previously in the section on costs that some RFID applications may require physical changes within the library. The most significant change is usually the one necessary in order to accommodate a book return materials handling system. Even in those cases where materials move directly from a book return to a sorter, there may be room to accommodate the sorting equipment. Some libraries choose to move materials on conveyors throughout the library, even between floors. Generally speaking, such systems are possible only when they are part of new building design or renovation.

Libraries that are replacing EM or RF security gates with RFID gates should find the restrictions on the latter to be much the same as the former. Security pedestals should not be placed in proximity to metal door frames (usually a 2-foot separation is recommended) and they should be no closer than 8 feet from computers and other electronic hardware.

As we discussed in the above section concerning costs, the movement to patron self service, both for check out and check in, has ramifications for the physical design of the library. As part of the effort to direct patrons to self check-out, some libraries have altogether eliminated circulation and check-out desks, replacing them with information desks. In some cases, they have transformed a circulation desk into a self check-out desk, keeping one staff person on the opposite side to assist patrons where necessary. Others have opted for the supermarket self-check design: a cluster of freestanding units with a single freestanding staff station in front.

Librarians also need to consider the following details of physical locations.

Location of book drop.

The book drop can be stand alone or built into the wall. The book drop can be used with or without a sorting conveyor. The number of sorting bins or book trucks used for the sorting conveyor system depends on the library's circulation statistics. When designing the sorting area, librarians need to keep fire codes in mind.

Location of self check-out station.

The self check-out stations can be stand alone or built onto the circulation counter. If it is stand alone, the self check-out station should be close to the circulation counter. Though most vendors provide the self check-out station with a remote monitoring function, a self-check machine, close to the counter, is convenient for patrons who need assistance. The self-check station should be 12 feet from the RFID security gates. The self-check stations should be 6 feet from each other, and 6 feet from the circulation station/readers.

Location of staff circulation station.

The circulation station/reader should be in the circulation-counter area. It should be 12 feet from the RFID security gates. No metal should be in or around the circulation-station area.

Location of security gates.

See section of Security Gates in this chapter.

2.2.5 Organizational Concerns

As we noted above in our discussion of standards, individual libraries rarely exist in a vacuum. More often than not, a public library system migrates to RFID, one branch at a time. Even once the entire library system's collection is RFID tagged, accommodation must still be made for materials that come into the system from consortium members and inter-library loans. Thorough and regular communication among all the parties potentially affected, both in the long and the short term, is essential for achieving implementation success.

Library systems with more than one location that wish to implement RFID technology often desire to start with one or two libraries, migrating system wide over a period of time. See Appendix A "Answers to Frequently Asked Questions" for information about organizational concerns.

Conclusion.

As noted above, librarians consider concerns as challenges; however, where there are challenges there are solutions. In fact, a standard data model of the tag may provide us with more solutions. In the following section we are going to discuss the Danish data model, which is the first RFID data model for libraries.

2.3 RFID DATA MODEL

A data model defines the requirements for data elements and data structure on the RFID tag. The data model discussed in this section is based on the "RFID Data Model for Libraries: Proposal for a Data Model" proposed by the Danish Libraries' RFID Working Group in July 2005 (RFID Data Model for Libraries Working Group, 2005). Discussion of this "RFID Data Model for Libraries" was permitted by the chairman of Danish Standard S24 (S24 is Committee on Information and Documentation).

On November 16, 2004, Danish Standards hosted a meeting for library suppliers who use RFID technology, organized by S24 subcommittee on technical interoperability. The meeting participants discussed the need for standardization of library RFID applications and the need for establishing a Working Group on a data model in library RFID applications (Danish Standards Association, 2005). The Working Group was chaired by Morten Hein, member of the S24 subcommittee.

On August 19, 2005, Leif Andresen, a library advisory officer of Danish National Library Authority (DNLA), chairman of DS S24, announced that the Danish RFID specification is available for discussion (RFID Data Model for Libraries Working Group, 2005).

He said, "This specification will be part of a Danish Standard Technical Report in some months by adding a Danish and an English summary. We now start a period with circulate the draft Technical Report among national standard bodies in Europe for consideration" (Andresen, 2005). The Technical Report will be published as DS/INF early 2006. In Finland the Working Group report has been reused with a few additions as a Finnish RFID for libraries' specification (see later in this section for more information on Finnish RFID data model).

Leif Andresen of the Danish National Library Authority wrote five functional requirements for RFID technology in Danish libraries (Andresen, 2004). In July 2005 the following five objectives were set for RFID in Danish libraries:

- For inter-library loan safeguarding an RFID tag from one library shall be readable and usable in other libraries.
- An RFID application shall have a standardized interface to any library system.
- To ensure independence of suppliers RFID tags shall be available from several sources.
- To ensure backward compatibility RFID tags shall use the same identification numbers as used on present bar-code systems
- Danish library RFID applications shall comply with existing international standards (RFID Data Model for Libraries Working Group, 2005).

The Working Group decided to develop a "One model for all purposes" data model that would work for all libraries without modifications. The structure of this data model has a mandatory part and an optional part covering four main areas: data elements, values and range, encoding, and physical mapping.

2.3.1 Data Elements

The core area of the data model is the data elements, which can be expressed in Table 2.1.

The data elements are clearly expressed by the Table 2.1. The version number is also a part of the data elements. To ensure compatibility between the first and later version, a version number is introduced as a data element (RFID Data Model for Libraries Working Group, 2005). In the next section we will discuss the values and range of the data elements.

2.3.2 Values and Range

The data model defines three types of data elements. They are mandatory data elements, structured extension data blocks, and unstructured extension data blocks. The mandatory

Table 2.1. RFID data elements.

Content Category	Mandatory Part	Structured Extension	Unstructured Extension
Meta data	AFI Standard version Check method Type of usage		Not defined
Item data	Primary item ID Number of parts in item Ordinal part number	Alternative item ID	Not defined

Libarary data	Country of owner
	    library
	Owner library
		Extended owner
		    library
			Not defined

Application data	None	Media format	Not defined
Supplier data	None	Supplier ID Item identification Order number Invoice number	Not defined

data elements include type of usage, number of parts in an item, ordinal part number, primary item ID, Cyclic Redundancy Check (CRC), country of owner library, and owner library. The structured extension data blocks include media format, alternative item ID, extended owner library code, supplier ID, item identification, order number, and invoice number. The unstructured extension data blocks are not defined yet.

Type of usage.
RFID tags can be used in acquisition, circulating items, noncirculating items, discarded items, and patron cards assigned values of 0, 1, 2, 7, and 8 respectively. Table 2.2 shows the type of usage.

Number of parts in an item.
The number of parts is used for package handling. It identifies the total number of the parts in the package. For example, DVD "God Father" has six discs with a booklet. The number of parts would be seven.

Table 2.2. Type of usage.

Type of Usage	Values and Range
Acquisition	0
Circulating items	1
Noncirculating items	2
Discarded items	7
Patron cards	8

Ordinal part number.

The ordinal part number is used for package handling. It identifies the number in an ordered sequence in the package. It could be one tag for each item in a package or the only one tag for the package. For example, DVD God Father with a single disc would have value "1" for both "Number of parts in item" and "Ordinal part number." For DVD God Father with three discs with a booklet, however, depending on a given library's policy, the ordinal part number could be one tag for the whole package, or could be four tags for a booklet and for each disk in the package, or could be no tag on a booklet and three tags for discs. The details of the scenario are in the following:

The elements of "Number of parts in an item" and "Ordinal part number" have one byte for possibility of 256 options in a media package.

DVD God Father with a single disk (one tag)
Number of parts in item = 1
Ordinal part number = 1

DVD God Father with three discs with a booklet (4 tags)
Number of parts in item = 4 (Total number of parts is 4.)
Ordinal part number = 1 (in tag 1)
Ordinal part number = 2 (in tag 2)
Ordinal part number = 3 (in tag 3)
Ordinal part number = 4 (in tag 4, booklet)

DVD God Father with three disks with a booklet (3 tags for each disc)
Number of parts in item = 4 (Total number of parts in item is 4.)
Ordinal part number = 1 (in tag 1)
Ordinal part number = 2 (in tag 2)
Ordinal part number = 3 (in tag 3)

DVD God Father with three disks with a booklet (1 tag)
Number of parts in item = 4
Ordinal part number = 0

The above two features are very useful for bound periodicals. For example, Chicago State University Library applies a tag to each issue. "Number of parts in item" and "Ordinal part number" can identify the total issues and the sequence in the bound periodical.

Primary item ID.

This data model recommends a transfer of current bar code as a unique identification number, with a maximum of 16 characters.

Redundancy Check.

The CRC is a self-checking technique to obtain data reliability. The 16-bit CRC is used for error detection in data communication (RFID Data Model for Libraries Working Group, 2005).

Country of owner library.

It is a two-character country code specified in ISO 3166-1 Alpha2 and it is the first part of the International Standard Identifier for Libraries and Related Organizations (ISIL) code.

Owner library.

This is the second part of the ISIL code. It is the national part of the ISIL code with 9 to 11 bytes in length. Libraries with a short ISIL code can use 9 bytes in the "Library Identifier" part. The ISIL code is specified in ISO 15511. The purpose of ISO 15511:2003 is to define and promote the use of a set of standard identifiers for the unique identification of libraries and related organizations, with a minimum impact on already existing systems.

The mandatory part of the chip layout of mandatory starting blocks can be summarized as Table 2.3:

Table 2.3.   Chip layout of mandatory starting block.

Offset	Length	Field
0 bit 0..3	4 bit	Version
0 bit 4..7	4 bit	Type of usage
1	1 byte	Parts in item
2	1 byte	Part number
3	16 bytes	Primary item ID
19	2 bytes	CRC
21	2 bytes	Country of owner library
23	9 or 11 bytes	Owner library
32 or 34		

The above data elements are mandatory. The following are the structured extension data blocks. Though the structured extension data blocks include media format, alternative item ID, extended owner library, supplier ID, item identification, order number, and invoice number, we only discuss three values that relate to the circulation operations.

Media format.

It is an item type code used to assist automatic sorting processes for returned books. The formats are defined as book, CD/DVD, magnetic tape (video or music), and very small item that requires special handling. Table 2.4 illustrates media format values.

Alternative item ID.

It is used for the primary ID code that is more than 16 characters.

Table 2.4.   Media format values.

Media Format	Values
Undefined	0
Book	1
CD/DCD/etc	2
Magnetic tape (video or music)	3
Other	4
Other, careful handling is required	5
Very small item, special handling may be required with sorting equipment	6

Extended owner library code.

It is used for long "owner library" codes. The optional data elements are supplier ID, item identification, order number, and invoice number. These fields assist processes between the library and the vendors. They could be decided by the library and/or the vendors/suppliers.

Unstructured extension data elements are not specified and these fields will be controlled by the library or vendors/suppliers.

2.3.3 Encoding

The Danish RFID Working Group decides to use (1) fields with fixed length to save space and to speed up reading and writing procedures according to the test (see appendix Danish Working Group Test for detailed information), (2) UTF8 as the encoding format, and (3) starting and ending information for each data block.

The encoding of RFID tags is a delicate job. The space available in a tag is still rather limited for the cost conscious buyer and vendor. This could tempt several to introduce very compressed encoding to save space. The Working Group has the position that some saving can be achieved by very compressed encoding, but the compressed encoding is rather short sighted. To ensure a longer life span for the coming data model it is the observation of the Working Group that coding principles shall follow practice from other application areas. Coding will, with a few exceptions, be 8 bit coding using ISO 8859-1 (Latin 1). (RFID Data Model for Libraries Working Group, 2005).

Some experts think this data model has a significant potential problem if more than bar-code information is to be stored on the RFID tags. The author thinks that all libraries will benefit from more than bar-code information, which is to be stored on the RFID tags, and benefit from the Danish model in the long run. For example, the Chicago State University Library applies a tag to each issue of the periodicals. "Number of parts in item" and "Ordinal part number" in the Danish RFID Data Model can identify the total issues and the sequence of the issue in the bound periodical. While the Danish RFID Data Model contributes to all libraries, there is one drawback for libraries that implemented the RFID before the adoption of this model. The drawback is potential retagging the collection. The potential problem lies in the earlier tags that do not have enough memory required by this data model. For example, Chicago State University implemented the RFID technology in 2003 with the tags memory of 16 bytes, whereas the data model requires 32 bytes. Shall the CSU Library retag its collections? If not retag, how could the CSU Library be interoperable with other libraries in its consortia and the rest of the world?

2.3.4 Physical Mapping

Physical mapping can influence the efficiency in reading from a particular data model including its encoding. Physical mapping of a tag is necessary in order to increase accuracy and speed of reading and writing.

2.3.5 Application Family Identifiers (AFIs)

To differentiate RFID tags used for other purposes, ISO had defined a standard called an Application Family Identifier (AFI). AFI allows RFID readers to filter the tags quickly. The AFI is a standard for RFID readers and enables reflected signals from tags to be distinguished among tags using different numbering schemes and different RFID applications. For example, a library book with a library AFI (checked out value of 0x9D) will not trigger the alarm system at Barns and Noble. This AFI identifier allows for more efficient and accurate use of tags in a global, multi RFID applications environment.

Danish library has proposed two library AFIs, that is, checked out (0x9D), and checked in (0x9E). They encourage libraries and vendors from other countries to use the same value.

2.3.6 Security

The Working Group recommends using AFI method for security—checked-in value 0x9E. The security system calls for tags with AFI value "checked in." If any tag responds the alarm sets off. The AFI security function is a specified part of ISO 15693-3.

Currently libraries are using non-AFI security systems. The Working Group identifies three different approaches of security systems, (1) server method, (2) magnetic strip method (a non-RFID method), and (3) the EAS bit method. EAS stands for Electronic Article Surveillance, which has been in use since 1960s. It is a loss-prevention technology using passive RFID surveillance. When a book is checked out from a library, the security bit on the tag is turned off. When patrons pass through the gates, the tag responds only if the item has not been checked out.

Though it is up to the library to choose its security mechanism, the Working Group suggests an AFI be used to identify the library RFID applications and for unique security method for a multitude of cooperating libraries.

The Danish Working Group includes the ALA's Resolution on Radio Frequency Identification and Privacy Principles in its Appendix (RFID Data Model for Libraries Working Group, 2005).

2.3.7 Inventory Performance versus Memory Size

The Danish Working Group tested inventory performance versus read memory size, because the inventory is the most demanding operation of speed and accuracy of reading. Tagsys, Bibliotheca, and FKI were involved in the test. They chose 40 books with a total length of 33cm. Tagsys LHA1 hand-held antenna and LHR2 inventory reader were used in the tests. All tags and equipment are compliant to ISO 18000-3, Mode 1.

The first test was inventory time versus read memory size. Given success read rate of 100%, as the memory size was increased from 64 bits to 256 bits, 512 bits, 896 bits, and the time to read the full row of books increased. Consequently, the speed of moving the hand-held antenna had to be reduced to ensure reliable reading. Table 2.5 shows the results of this test.

Table 2.5.   Inventory time and speed vs. read memory size.

Memory Size (bits)	Read Time (ms)	Speed (books/sec)
64	1380	29
256	1950	20.5
512	2780	14.4
896	4530	8.8

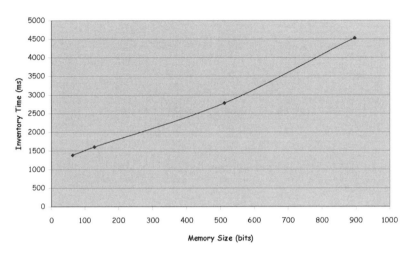

Figure 2.1. Inventory time vs. memory size (bits).

Figure 2.1 illustrates the relationship between inventory time and memory size (bits).

The second test was success read rate versus read memory size. Given the reading speed at 24 cm/sec, as the memory size increased, there was an increasing degradation in reading rate. Table 2.6 displays the results of the second test.

Figure 2.2 shows the graphic of the Table 2.6.

The Working Group concluded that the transfer of increasing amounts of memory data affects inventory performance. They recommend that libraries minimize memory transfer required for inventory operation.

2.3.8 Other Data Models

The Finnish Data Model.

On November 24, 2005, the Finnish Libraries' RFID Working Group announced its final version of the Finnish Data Model (Finnish Libraries' RFID Working Group, 2005). The Finnish Libraries' RFID Working Group was established in spring 2005. The plan was to evaluate existing standards and recommendations, and use these as the starting point. After the evaluation, the group agreed to build the Finnish Data Model,

Table 2.6. Success read rate vs. memory size.

Memory Size (bits)	Books Read	Success Read Rate (%)
64	40	100
256	33.4	83.5
512	25	62.5
896	18.4	46

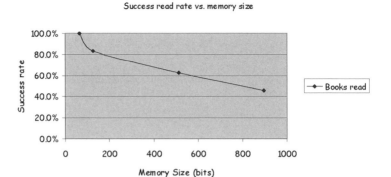

Figure 2.2. Success read rate vs. memory size.

using the brilliant work done in Denmark as the starting point. Key differences between the Finnish and Danish specification are the following:

- Request to write protect the mandatory data elements in order to improve security
- Request to use neither the alternate item ID nor extended owner library since these data elements are not write protected, due to being located in the (non–write protected) structured extension data blocks
- Recommendation to limit the utilization of Type-of-usage code
- Recommendation to store MARC media type code into unstructured extension data block 101

This specification is maintained by the Helsinki University Library—The National Library of Finland (Finnish Libraries' RFID Working Group, 2005).

The American Model and the National Information Standards Organization (NISO) Working Group.

The most recent information of the American model and the NISO Working Group of RFID can be found in Dr. Chachra's presentation (Chachra, 2005) and at the Web site of the BISG (Book Industry Study Group, 2005).

On October 25 and 26, 2005, NISO and University of North Texas cosponsored an RFID institute "RFID Technologies: Standards and Integration in the Information Environment" at Denton, Texas. The speakers are mixed with experts of the RFID industry and librarians. The following discussion highlights the key points of the NISO Working Group.

The NISO RFID Institute (Chachra, 2005) discussed goals of the NISO Working Group. They are (1) identify specific NISO activities or standards that would make the application of RFID technology most effective for its community; (2) identify related standards work where NISO might partner; and (3) identify points where RFID issues could be integrated within other NISO standards work. The participants of the Working Group are RFID hardware manufacturers, RFID software vendors, RFID Library users, and book jobbers/vendors and other related organizations. The NISO Working Group identified four important issues (Chachra, 2005): privacy, support of functional capabilities, performance efficiency, and costs. Chachra mentioned that the NISO Working Group is to examine existing standards and existing data models.

The NISO Working Group is now studying the Danish data model. The results of this study could be, 1) the model meets the needs of USA RFID applications; (2) the model meets the needs of USA applications with some modifications; and (3) a new model will have to be developed to meet our needs. Based on the outcome of the study, a course of action for the future will be defined (Chachra, 2005). The timetable for this study is approximately 6 months. It is expected that the American data model will be announced at the annual conference of the American Library Association in June 2006.

Conclusion.

Data model is a standard for both libraries and vendors. With a data model we do not have to worry about the use of proprietary standards. With a data model more librarians or library administrators will consider implementing the RFID technology in their libraries.

2.4   IMPORTANT ISSUES

There are a number of important issues that need further discussion from different angles with additional information, though some of them might be briefly discussed in the above sections. The issues that deserve extended discussion are privacy, library policies and procedures, security gates, and comparison of library RFID versus mainstream RFID.

2.4.1   Privacy

There are trade-offs between technology advantages and privacy. As the technology is refined, more pervasive and possibly invasive uses for RFID tags are in the works. The use of RFID technology has engendered considerable controversy because people perceive that the tag on the book could be used to trace a patron's reading habits, whereas the tag in a library patron card could reveal a person's data. However, there should be more privacy concerns of ILS systems or any information systems than from RFID tags. As long as libraries follow the ALA Guidelines when implementing the RFID, privacy concerns should not be a problem.

The RFID technology brings libraries advantages and also concerns about privacy. "The [ALA] Intellectual Freedom Committee (IFC), the Office for Intellectual Freedom (OIF), and the Office for Information Technology Policy (OITP) joined the Book Industry Study Group (BISG), a nonprofit research group comprised of organizations from all sectors of the publishing industry, to form a Working Group dedicated to influencing how RFID technology will be employed in that industry and in libraries" (Oliver, 2005).

RFID patron cards can speed up the circulation process; however, some have expressed privacy concerns by using RFID patron cards. If your library decides to use RFID patron cards, it would be a good idea to keep less information on the patron card and more information in the ILS database. In this way, users can have more protection of their personal information.

BISG RFID privacy principles.

All businesses, organizations, libraries, educational institutions, and nonprofits that buy, sell, loan, or otherwise make available books and other content to the public utilizing RFID technologies shall

1. implement and enforce an up-to-date organizational privacy policy that gives notice and full disclosure as to the use, terms of use, and any change in the terms of use for data collected via new technologies and processes, including RFID;

2. insure that no personal information is recorded on RFID tags that may contain a variety of transactional data;

3. protect data by reasonable security safeguards against interpretation by any unauthorized third party; and

4. comply with relevant federal, state, and local laws as well as industry best practices and policies.

Insure that the four principles outlined above are verifiable by an independent audit (BISG, 2005).

The year 2005 reads the draft of the "Guidelines for Implementing RFID Technologies in Libraries: Privacy and Intellectual Freedom Concerns" (American Library Association, 2005), which will be referred to as the ALA Guidelines in the remainder of this chapter. The ALA Guidelines suggest libraries should only store the item number on the tag, encrypt the data on the tag, and the item number is not searchable in libraries' OPAC. Meanwhile the RFID card for workplace access is already in widespread use in corporations using RFID systems to control access to their facilities. The access card may store more personal information than a library patron card.

At Chicago State University Library, Dean McCrank discussed the possibility of using RFID patron cards to control library building access and other purposes. The ALA Guidelines suggest refraining from storing personal data on patron cards/tags, and suggest using dual patron cards, that is, RFID cards or traditional cards (could be magnetic-strip cards or bar-code cards depending on the institution). How could the Chicago State University Library conquer this dilemma? Actually, it could be implemented according to the ALA Guidelines. A patron has a choice to use or not use the RFID patron card. Each patron has an institutional ID, or a patron bar code, which can be stored on the patron card. This simple solution is safe and secure.

Library patrons are afraid the RFID tag used in books and other library materials may actively monitor them at home. Tags on some returned books are torn off or damaged (the chip was scraped off the tag). They thought the RFID tag tracked wherever they went, or someone on the street with an RFID reader could find what books they checked out. Although the mainstream RFID technology is used for tracking, the purpose of the library RFID system is not designed for tracking. The RFID tag on the book functions as a bar code or pointer to the ILS system. The RFID tag ID has no use without ILS. Anyone with a reader that wants to track you has to be very close to you, that is, 6 inches to read the RFID tags. The only information he gets from the tag is the item number (bar code). Almost no library in the world allows patrons to search item number in OPAC. This means that even if a stranger on the street has the item numbers of your books, he or she cannot find out the titles of the books. The fear of privacy invasion stems from a lack of knowledge about RFID systems.

The ALA Guidelines suggest libraries construct policies and procedures to protect library users' privacy in compliance with the ALA Code of Ethics. Librarians need to let users know that the information on the RFID tag is only used for circulation and stack management purposes. Lawrence McCrank, the Dean of the Chicago State University Library, thinks that privacy is a sociopolitical issue, which requires sociopolitical solutions. He asked librarians to consider that the benefits of RFID may outweigh the drawbacks.

Given that RFID will be included on everything, from refrigerators and passports, there may be bigger things to worry about than tagging books. Laura Smart commented on Dr. McCrank's presentation (McCrank, 2005) in her blog: "I'm still not convinced that the benefits will override the potential erosion of my civil liberties but McCrank made an appealing pitch by shifting the focus of RFID in libraries from collections to users. I do agree with McCrank when he says that in order to remain relevant, librarians will have to accept that ubiquitous computing will be part and parcel of our environment. We need to come up with intelligent solutions to the problems so we can derive the advantages of RFID" (Smart, 2005, June). Legislation may be one of the solutions to privacy issues.

Several states are considering legislation that would pose restrictions on the use of RFID by retailers and libraries. It is, therefore, important to monitor legislative activity and be prepared to inform legislators about the differences between retail and library applications. Library administrators should be sure to keep their boards informed (Boss, 2004).

Laws and legislation.

Are there laws and legislation governing the RFID? The U.S. Federal Trade Commission (FTC) and Congress have begun hearings to consider the regulation of RFID frequency bands and other related issues.

Existing property rights and common law privacy torts substantially limit the potential abuse of RFID. Putting a chip or a reader on a person or person's property against his/her will is a tort violation of constitutional rights and fundamental liberties, which is certainly a criminal offense. Hiding RFID readers in one's house or car would be no different than wiretapping one's phone or hiding a video camera in one's kitchen. An RFID reader is much easier to locate than a wiretap because it operates at a known, easily detectible frequency. (Sweeney, 2005)

Joe Simitian, California State Senator, proposed 3-year moratorium on RFID-enabled ID cards. He asked a fundamental question: What are the specific kinds of information that should be encoded on RFID-enabled ID cards? Most of the concerns expressed to date have been over hypothetical applications and equally hypothetical potentials for abuse (RFID_LIB listserv, 2005). Existing uses of RFID in library are designed to benefit both the user and the library. The RFID library patron card contains only an institution number corresponding to the patron's information in the ILS, only accessible by authorized library staff. To prevent the strangers on the street from reading your card, you simply need to wrap the library patron card in aluminum foil.

Besides California, several other states have also proposed RFID related legislation. Even though the purpose of the RFID related legislation is slightly different, the main focus is to protect consumers' privacy and rights, and to prevent abuses of the RFID technology. The legislation is described as Right to Know style regulation, requiring disclosure for tagged consumer products (SecureID news, 2005). The following is a summary of the pending RFID related legislation (Legislative info, 2005):

Massachusetts – HB 1447, SB 181
PURPOSE: Requires labels regarding use and purpose of RFID on consumer products. Requires the ability to remove tags; and restricts information on tags to inventory and like purposes.

Maryland – HB 354
PURPOSE: Creates a task force to study privacy and other issues related to RFID and report on whether legislation is needed.

Missouri – SB 128
PURPOSE: Requires a conspicuous label on consumer packaging with RFID disclosing existence of the tag and that the tag can transmit a unique ID before and after purchase.

Nevada – AB 264
PURPOSE: Requires manufacturers, retailers and others to ensure placement of a label regarding existence of RFID on product prior to sale.

New Hampshire – HB 203
PURPOSE: Requires written or verbal notice of existence of a tracking device on any product prior to sale.

New Mexico – HB 215
PURPOSE: Requires businesses purveying tagged items to post notices on their premises and labels on the products; requires removal or deactivation of tag at point of sale.

Rhode Island – H 5929
PURPOSE: Prohibits state or local government from using RFID to track movement or identity of employees, students or clients or others as a condition of a benefit or service.

South Dakota – HB 1114
PURPOSE: Prohibits requiring a person to receive implant of an RFID chip.

Tennessee – HB 300, SB 699
PURPOSE: Requires conspicuous labeling of goods containing RFID disclosing existence of RFID and that it can transmit unique information.

Utah – HB 185
PURPOSE: Amends computer crime law to include RFID.

Texas – HB 2953
PURPOSE: Prohibits school district from requiring student to use an RFID device for identification; requires school to provide alternative method to those who object to RFID.

Privacy activists.

Privacy activists have been opposing the RFID technology. You may find more information at http://www.spychips.com/index.html. Tien expressed his concerns that tags are often promiscuous, offering no protection against unauthorized reading. Tien said that tags threaten privacy:

1. Tag readability is stealthy—you will not know it is happening.
2. Tags are remotely readable.
3. Tags can contain much information.
4. Even tags with no personally identifiable information (PII) often contain a static, unique ID number. Tags with unique IDs can easily be associated with a person's true identity (Tien, 2005).

The following are the arguments that do not agree with Tien's privacy concerns:

1. A passive tag's read range is within 6 inches by a regular reader. You will know if it happens.
2. The distance of the remote readability is within 6 inches by a regular reader. No one considers 6 inches as remote.
3. The RFID passports and drivers' licenses may contain much information. A library tag for an item only contains a bar-code number. There is no personal data on the tag. A library tag for

a patron contains an institution ID or a patron bar-code number. There is no other personal data on the tag.

4. Most libraries use RFID for collections, not for patrons. Therefore, there is no association with a person's true identity.

The ALA guidelines minimize the privacy concerns.

The following ALA suggestions may cover all the above issues:
Libraries utilizing "smart cards" should use an "opt-in" system that allows library users to choose between "smart cards" and bar code enabled cards in order to accommodate users who do not wish to utilize or carry an RFID-enabled device (American Library Association, 2005).

The following ALA suggestions may cover one to three of the above issues:
Libraries should educate and inform library users concerning RFID technology and its current and future use in the library.
Libraries should train staff to protect user privacy.
Libraries should affirm and reinforce their obligation to secure bibliographic and patron database from unauthorized entry (American Library Association, 2005).

The following ALA suggestions may cover issues one and three:
Libraries should limit the information stored on the tag to the item's bar code.
Libraries should refrain from storing personally identifiable information (PII) on RFID tags or RFID-enabled patron cards.
Libraries should encrypt information stored on RFID tags (American Library Association, 2005).

The following ALA suggestions may cover issue one:
In relation to their use of RFID technologies, libraries should recognize their institutional obligations with respect to notice, access, use, disclosure, retention, enforcement, security, and disposal of records.
Libraries should disclose any changes in their privacy policies or in terms of use for patron data that may result from the adoption of an RFID system.
Libraries should clearly identify all RFID readers so that users know they are in use (American Library Association, 2005).

The following ALA suggestions may cover issue two:
Libraries should not grant individuals the ability to search the library's catalog by bar-code number, in order to avoid linking specific information to a specific user (American Library Association, 2005).
In conclusion we can say that the ALA Guidelines minimize the privacy concerns of patrons. All libraries that implement the RFID technology should follow the ALA Guidelines.

Are librarians front runners?

Librarians have been doing an excellent job of raising awareness of RFID privacy issues, and discussing the issues with concerned parties. Jim Lichtenberg, a library IT consultant, stated that libraries were ahead of the pack and that the lessons libraries had learned could provide guidance to others. Libraries are much further along utilizing RFID in a consumer environment than anyone else, and represent a wonderful test bed in which to work through the issues of RFID because they have such profound concerns about the rights of their patrons (Lichtenberg, 2004).

In summary, patrons, students, and faculty should be informed if the library is using the RFID technology. The key to privacy issues is education. As Robkin said, for librarians one way to deal with privacy issues is to educate staff as well as patrons regarding

RFID privacy (Robkin, 2005). When users understand RFID along with its benefits and disadvantages, they will make intelligent choices regarding the privacy issues.

2.4.2   Library Policies and Procedures

It is necessary to develop and establish the library RFID policy prior to implementation of the RFID technology. You may start from the "Guidelines for Implementing RFID Technologies in Libraries: Privacy and Intellectual Freedom Concerns" (American Library Association, 2005) and adopt its recommendations to fit into your own library policies.

The ALA Guidelines recommend limiting information on the tag, meaning less vulnerability to the patron from hackers and intruders. Both the Danish RFID Working Group and the ALA suggest a bar-code number on the tag. The bar code cannot reveal a book title without information from the ILS, which is accessed only by library staff. Furthermore, the bar code cannot be searched in the OPAC.

The ALA recommendation is consistent with the recommendation of the Danish Working Group. The American RFID Working Group has been working on its RFID data model. We expect to see the first draft from the American RFID Working Group in 2006. More information on the American RFID Working Group is available in the section of Standards in this chapter.

A consortia policy and procedure should also be discussed and established. In order to eliminate challenges of compatibility and interoperability, the consortia need to be proactive to have policies and procedures in place before the first library in the consortia implements RFID technology. A consortium recommended vendor is very useful. It can eliminate the problems of interoperability. A consortium negotiation of purchasing can lower the RFID price (Haley & Lewis, 2004).

In a consortium environment, libraries using RFID need to continue using bar-codes and bar-code equipment for inter-library loan and reciprocal borrowing. A consortium needs to support both bar code and RFID for many years to come (Haley & Lewis, 2004).

Most libraries implement RFID incrementally, that is, one collection at a time. The RFID library should continue supporting bar codes. The same principle applies to the library consortia. One library in a consortia implemented that the RFID should continue using bar codes for inter-library loan and reciprocal borrowing.

2.4.3   Security Gates

In this section, the words RFID security gates, security systems, and pedestals are used interchangeably.

We will start this section with two terms: EAS and AFI. EAS stands for Electronic Article Surveillance systems, which was developed in the 1960s. It is a loss-prevention technology using passive RFID surveillance. When a book is checked out, the security bit on the tag is turned off. When patrons pass through the gates, the tag activates the alarm if the item has not been checked out. AFI stands for Application Family Identifier. AFI is used to distinguish between tags using different numbering schemes and/or different RFID applications. For example, a library DVD with a library AFI (checked out value of 0x9D) will not trigger the alarm system at BlockBuster, and vice versa.

This AFI identifier allows for more efficient and accurate use of tags in a global, multi RFID applications environment.

There are four different types of security systems. They are (1) server security systems, (2) magnetic-strip security systems (a non-RFID method), (3) EAS bit security systems, and (4) AFI security systems. The AFI system is currently unavailable to the library RFID market. The EAS security systems are now the most popular on the market. AFI security systems will most likely dominate the market in the future when the library AFI becomes ISO standards.

Libraries have the choice of using traditional magnetic gates or RFID gates. Any library can use magnetic gates, no matter which library RFID vendor you choose. However, the server security systems approach and the EAS approach are tied to specific vendors. There are very few vendors using the server security systems approach; however, there are many vendors using the EAS approach. The AFI security systems approach is new and will most likely become an ISO standard in the future.

Accuracy and speed are very important factors in RFID security gates. When patrons with checked-out books pass through the gates, the readers need to broadcast and receive data very quickly and accurately. It is a challenge for RFID technology as many patrons with multiple checked-out items pass through the security gates. The security system must insure an accurate and fast read. It is important to insure that the wake-up and read commands are both issued rapidly. Pedestal antennas should not face each other; instead they should point 25 to 45 degrees relative to the gate and in the direction of outgoing patrons. As many tags are in the gate area simultaneously, collision is a concern. Libraries should tune the pedestal reader to read every tag correctly. Interference is another concern. When installing security gates, librarians need to think carefully about the location for security gates. The RFID security gates should be close to a circulation counter. This increases staff efficiency in handling alarms and checking patrons leaving the area. The security gates should be 12 feet away from the self-check station, 12 feet away from the circulation station/reader, and 12 feet away from the stacks. There should be at least 18 inches between the door and the security gates with no metal around the security gates area.

Boss (2004) discussed the problems of security gates. He stated that while the short range readers used for circulation charge, discharge, and inventorying appear to read the tags 100% of the time, the performance of the security gates is more problematic (Boss 2004). Before the Chicago State University Library implemented RFID, librarians at the CSU Library visited an RFID equipped library and did some tests on the EAS security gate. Two or more items with checked-in status passed through the security gate and triggered the alarm when the tags did not overlap each other, that is, the RFID tags were held in different positions so that they did not interfere with each other. When two or more item tags were overlapped, the security gate was not triggered. Therefore, the books could be stolen from the library. We tested the tags in two books separated by 5 cm, 10 cm, 15 cm and 20 cm. We drew the conclusion that tags must be separated by at least 20 cm in order to eliminate RF interference.

Librarians need to not only consider the gates' accuracy and speed, but also pay attention to keeping the gate areas clean, dry, and within normal temperature ranges. As stated in the section on "Readers," extreme heat, humidity, and direct sunlight may affect the RFID security gates' performance.

Hopefully as RFID technology matures, a more sophisticated security gate system will be available, and more standards will be established.

2.4.4   Library RFID versus Mainstream RFID

Mainstream RFID technology has been mainly used for supply chains and retailers. It is much more complicated than library RFID technology. The mainstream RFID technology provides visibility "from the receiving dock, to the production line, to transportation vehicles, and even to the retail store shelves" (Sweeney, 2005, p 208). However, the library RFID technology is simple data exchange that focuses on circulation and its related functions, that is, stack management, inventory, automatic check in, automatic sorting, self check, and security gates. Currently, a library book is not traced from publisher, to vendor, to transportation vehicles, to the library, to another inter-library loan, or to the patron. Mainstream RFID technology shares data with partners, whereas libraries share RFID data with inter-library loan and reciprocal borrowing.

The inventory function of the mainstream RFID technology is dynamic, whereas the library RFID inventory is static. For example, the Wal-Mart RFID system knows that one store has 100 plasma TVs coming through the door. Shipping and receiving links this information to point-of-sale data. The mainstream RFID system collects inventory information and automatically generates orders to its supply chain when inventory levels drop below a certain point (Sweeney, 2005). The library RFID inventory function is used once a year to scan and collect data on shelves and compare it with the data in the ILS database. The library RFID inventory function is neither linked to the point of check-out data, nor is it for replenishment.

The mainstream RFID technology takes advantage of real time, item level data and provides continuous inventory data capture. The library RFID technology simplifies the circulation processes, especially in the areas of automatic check in and sorting processes, and reduces inventory time. It only deploys a fraction of the mainstream RFID technology. The mainstream RFID technology uses open RFID systems, which enable retailers and suppliers to share information, whereas the library RFID technology is a closed system, which relies on an ILS.

Publishers think about RFID for inventory management, tracking materials through the production process, and support for supply-chain dynamics of shipping and logistics. How long these tags would stay "alive" in retail use touches on postsale benefits in that environment (Lichtenberg, 2005). Librarians think about how to use publishers' RFID tag data for libraries' acquisition records, how to add unique item ID to publishers' RFID tags, and how to use it for inter-library loans.

RFID could be the next big thing. Challenges include privacy, lower price, development of standards, and development of new levels of middleware to manage RFID. Librarians and booksellers have different needs. Librarians want persistent chips with long life spans, while retail operations want chips they can kill, or neutralize, at the point of sale.

Conclusions about the decision to implement RFID.

The decision to move forward with RFID is one that each library must make based on multiple factors. A careful cost benefit study should be done in order to be sure that the benefits justify the up-front expense to the library and that there is an overall return on the investment made. The library must weigh its patrons' receptivity to new technology, its staff's ability to handle the change, the physical requirements of RFID, and all the other factors discussed in this chapter. Also under consideration must be the library's commitment to the continuing task of providing newer and better ways to assist patrons in accomplishing their primary goal—getting the right information and materials, in the most effective and efficient way possible.

This book is neither an RFID primer, nor a theoretical treatise. It provides information and guidance for librarians who must envision and/or implement RFID technology in their libraries. We hope that this chapter has served this purpose.

REFERENCES

American Library Association. (2005). *Guidelines for implementing RFID technologies in libraries: Privacy and intellectual freedom concerns.* Retrieved November 24, 2005, from http://www.ala.org/ala/oif/oifprograms/openhearings/relatedlinksabc/draftrfidguidelines.htm

Andresen, L. (2004). *Danish National Library Authority's strategy for RFID in libraries.* Retrieved September 21, 2005, from http://www.en.ds.dk/_root/scripts/getmedia.asp?media_id=1883

Andresen, L. (2005). *The Danish RFID specification.* Retrieved September 21, 2005, from http://litablog.org/?p=72#comments

Ayre, L.B. (2004). *RFID and libraries.* Retrieved November 24, 2005, from http://galecia.com/included/docs/rfid_position_paper_rev2.pdf

Bitner, L. (2005, October). *More than theft detection RFID challenges: A bookseller's perspective.* Paper presented at the NISO Texas Center for Digital Knowledge Institute: RFID Technologies: Standards and Integration in the Information Environment. Retrieved November 25, 2005, from http://www.txcdk.org/rfid/knowledge_base.php?cat=conf&detail=10#10

Book Industry Study Group. (2005). *RFID privacy principles.* Retrieved November 9, 2005, from http://www.bisg.org/

Boss, R. W. (2004). *RFID Technology for Libraries.* Retrieved March 7, 2005, from http://www.ala.org/ala/pla/plapubs/plapubs/technotes/rfidtechnology.htm

Chachra, V. (2005, October). *A report on NISO's work on RFID standards in libraries.* Paper presented at the NISO Texas Center for Digital Knowledge Institute: RFID Technologies: Standards and Integration in the Information Environment. Retrieved November 25, 2005, from http://www.txcdk.org/rfid/knowledge_base.php?cat=conf&detail=10#10

Danish Standards Association. (2005). *RFID Data Model for Libraries.* Retrieved October 19, 2005, from http://www.en.ds.dk/2567,1

Finnish Libraries' RFID Working Group. (2005, November). *RFID data model for libraries: Proposal for a data model : Based on the document prepared by the Danish RFID Data Model for Libraries Working Group.* Retrieved December 19, 2005, from http://www.lib.helsinki.fi/katve/toiminta/docs/RFID-DataModel-FI-20051124.pdf

Haley, C., & Lewis, J. (2004, April). *Implementation of radio frequency identification (RFID) technology in a Voyager library.* Poster session presented at the annual conference of the Voyager EndUser, Chicago, IL.

Legislative Info. (2005). Retrieved November 25, 2005, from http://www.libraryrfid.net/wordpress/index.php?s=Legislative+info

Lichtenberg, J. (2004). *RFID, coming to a library near you.* Retrieved July 25, 2005, from http://www.resourceshelf.com/2004/10/rfid-coming-to-library-near-you_19.html

Lichtenberg, J. (2005). ALA/BISG Sponsored RFID Working Group Holds Berkeley Meeting. *Library Journal.* Retrieved September 25, 2005, from http://www.libraryjournal.com/article/CA512186.html

McCrank, L. J. (2005, June). *RFID in Chicago State University Library.* Paper presented at the Annual Conference of the American Library Association on the Radio Frequency Identification Technology in Libraries, Chicago, IL.

Mesenbrink, J. (2002). Shopping for RFID. *Security, 39*(8), 10–14.

Oliver, K. (2005). Proposed guidelines for implementing RFID technologies in libraries: privacy and intellectual freedom concerns. *Memorandum to ALA Executive Board.*

RFID Data Model for Libraries Working Group affiliated to Danish Standard S24/u4. (2005, July). *RFID data model for libraries: Proposal for a data model.* Retrieved October 19, 2005, from http://www.bs.dk/standards/RFID%20Data%20Model%20for%20Libraries.pdf

Robkin, S. (2005, June). *Real world RFID.* Paper presented at the Annual Conference of the American Library Association on the Radio Frequency Identification Technology in Libraries, Chicago, IL.

San Francisco Public Library Technology and Privacy Advisory Committee. (2005). *Radio Frequency Identification and the San Francisco Public Library: Summary report.* Retrieved December 5, 2005, from http://www.sfpl.org/librarylocations/libtechcomm/introduction-for-web.pdf

SecureID news. (2005). *A number of state legislatures consider RFID-related issues.* Retrieved November 30, 2005, from http://www.secureidnews.com/library/2005/11/01/a-number-of-state-legislatures-consider-rfidrelated-issues/

Shigo, K. (2003). Vernon to use TagSys RFID technology. *Computers in Libraries*, 23(5), 44.

Smart, L. J. (2005). Considering RFID: Benefits, limitations, and best practices. *C&RL News, 1* (2005), 13–16.

Smart, L. J. (2005, June). *Radio Frequency Identification technology in libraries: Meeting with the RFID experts.* Retrieved November 24, 2005, from http://litablog.org/?p=72

Sweeney, P. J., II. (2005). *RFID for dummies.* Indianapolis, IN: Wiley Publishing.

Tien, L. (2005, October). *RFID privacy & security concerns.* Paper presented at NISO Texas Center for Digital Knowledge Institute: RFID Technologies: Standards and Integration in the Information Environment. Retrieved November 25, 2005, from http://www.txcdk.org/rfid/knowledge_base.php?cat=conf&detail=10#10

Chapter 3

Tags, Readers, and Applications

This chapter discusses the tags, hardware, and software required when using RFID in libraries. Although this book is not intended to be a technical treatise, it is important to understand some basic information about how RFID works from a hardware and software perspective, specifically understanding tags, readers, security gates, and automated return systems, in order to learn which options will be the best fit for the library's needs. The library must determine the functionality it requires and choose not only the right hardware, but also the software that is compatible with the hardware that offers the desired features. Some thought must be given to the library's goals and objectives when making a decision to purchase RFID in order to realize the promise it offers. Specifically, we will address the following:

- Tags
- Readers
- Conversion stations
- Staff circulation stations
- Patron self check-out stations
- Automated returns and sorting
- Electronic Article Surveillance (EAS) and security gates
- Stack maintenance
- The Reader/ILS Interface

We begin the discussion of hardware with RFID tags, the basis for all RFID technology.

Figure 3.1. A library RFID tag consists of a laminated label with an antenna and a chip (reproduced by permission of Tagsys).

3.1 TAGS

Regardless of the manufacturer or RFID system, all RFID tags used in libraries operate at a high frequency (HF) of 13.56 MHz. As opposed to "active" tags that are used in other RFID environments, such as highway toll collection, tags used in libraries are classified as "passive" because they have no built-in battery to provide power. Instead, they have tiny chips (semiconductors) that "wake up" in response to an RFID field generated by an external RFID reader. Since passive tags have no power source of their own, they must draw their energy from the reader's radio wave upon entering the interrogation zone. That said, there are many other features that differentiate one library RFID tag from another. These differences should be fully understood before choosing an RFID system and deciding what kind of tag to purchase. Consider the following:

- Compliance with standards (proprietary or nonproprietary)
- R/W (Read/Write) or WORM (Write Once Read Many)
- EAS capabilities
- Physical Construction
- Plain versus preprogrammed/preprinted tags
- Data structure, capacity, and content

3.1.1 Compliance with Standards

In this section we will look at the various standards organizations and how hardware vendors are incorporating the standards promoted by these organizations into their products. We will also look at how these standards apply specifically to libraries.

Standards organizations.
Standards have been established and continue to be developed by both international (such as ISO) and national (such as NISO) organizations. Of course, individual companies

Figure 3.2. A passive library tag.

often establish their own proprietary standards for emerging technologies. They can choose to share their proprietary intellectual property with those outside their companies. In some cases, these manufacturers attempt to have their internally developed standards incorporated into nationally or internationally recognized standards. However, until such time that a proprietary design or application is incorporated into a recognized standard, it should be considered proprietary.

The International Standardization Organization (ISO) is a network of the national standards institutes of approximately 150 countries, with a central office in Geneva, Switzerland. It coordinates the standards acceptance system and publishes the determined international standards. The National Information Standards Organization (NISO) does the same in the United States and has a membership composed of over 70 companies and organizations in the fields of publishing, libraries, information technology (IT), and media. The NISO has its headquarters in Bethesda, Maryland.

ISO has partnered with the International Electro-technical Commission (IEC) to set standards for RFID including the ISO 18000 RFID Air Interface Standards officially adopted in 2004. ISO 18000 standards, the very first to be designed specifically for RFID, have the goal of creating true global interoperability for communication between tags and readers, even at different frequencies (Sweeney, 2005). ISO has been working with experts and standards organizations and has developed a set of RFID protocols that are potentially relevant to libraries. Those standards are shown in Table 3.1, along with other ISO standards that relate to libraries (although not RFID specific).

Relevant standards for library RFID technology.

The goal of the RFID standards is to have interoperability of tags and readers that operate at the same frequency. As noted earlier, the frequency standard for libraries is 13.56 MHz. All products being sold to libraries operate at 13.56 MHz. ISO standards

Table 3.1. Relevant standards for library RFID technology.

Standard	Standard Number	Standard Name	Notes
ISO	3166-1:1997	Codes representing the names of countries and their subdivisions – Part 1: Country codes	
	10646:2003	Information technology – Universal Multiple-Octet Coded Character Set (UCS)	Use UCS transformation format 8 (UTF-8)
	15511:2003	Information and documentation – International Standard Identifier for Libraries and Related Organizations (ISIL)	The purpose of ISO 15511:2003 is to define and promote the use of a set of standard identifiers for the unique identification of libraries and related organizations with a minimum impact on already existing systems (ISO, 2003). For example the ISIL code for Melby Library in Denmark is DK-62 1104. The Library of Congress is responsible for the ISIL registration authority in USA.
	15961:2004	Information technology – Radio frequency identification (RFID) for item management – Data protocol: application interface	
	15962:2004	Information technology – Radio frequency identification (RFID) for item management – Data protocol: data encoding rules and logical memory functions	

Table 3.1. Continued.

Standard	Standard Number	Standard Name	Notes
	15963:2004	Information technology – Radio frequency identification for item management – Unique identification for RF tags	
	18000	Information technology – Radio frequency identification for item management	ISO 18000 has seven different parts. Only part 1 and part 3 are relevant to library RFID.
	18000-1:2004	Information technology – Radio frequency identification for item management – Part 1: Reference architecture and definition of parameters to be standardized	Part 1 is the system architecture for RFID for item management, including integration with legacy systems and interoperability.
	18000-3:2004	Information technology – Radio frequency identification for item management – Part 3: Parameters for air interface communications at 13,56 MHz	Part 3 enumerates two different modes of operation, which are not interoperable although they are designed not to interfere with each other. Mode 1 is based on ISO 15693 with improvements, and Mode 2 lays out a new high-speed communication option. ISO 18000 only addresses the air interface communication – how a tag and a reader communicate to each other. It neither defines the data structure nor the content of different tags.
ANSI/ NISO Standards Proprietary Standards	Z39.83:2002	NISO Circulation Interchange Protocol (NCIP) 3M Standard Interchange Protocol (SIP)	pt. 1. Protocol (NCIP) pt. 2. Protocol implementation

that relate specifically to this interoperability are ISO 18000-3 and ISO 15693. While the ISO 18000 standards are the first to be adopted specifically for RFID technology, they incorporate earlier standards that address related technologies.

18000-3 defines a standard set of communication guidelines for 13.56 MHz RFID tags. It incorporates the "prior art" of ISO 15693, a standard developed for contact-less access control cards. Although this standard addresses issues similar in certain respects to RFID, it does not contain precise guidelines for several RFID features. It should be noted that ISO 18000-3 enumerates two different modes of operation. These modes, while not interoperable, are designed not to interfere with one another. Mode 1 is based on ISO 15693 with some improvements. Mode 2 lays out a new high-speed communication option. The establishment of two modes as opposed to a single mode was done to meet the objections of manufacturers whose tags do not comply with the new high-speed communication option. Mode 1 of ISO 18000-3 allows vendors who offer ISO 15693 compliant tags to truthfully state that their tags meet the ISO 18000-3 standard established for RFID. Presumably, in time, the manufacturers of ISO 15693 compliant tags will incorporate the high-speed communications option so that a single mode with true interoperability will be all that remains.

Libraries are advised to ask their potential RFID vendors, not only what standards their tags comply with, but also, in the case of ISO 18000-3, which mode is used. At the time of this writing, most RFID tag manufacturers have not yet adopted Mode 2. For simplicity purposes, it is best to refer to tags as being ISO 18000-3 compliant only if they utilize Mode 2 while referring to Mode 1 compliant tags as ISO 15693. This nomenclature is the one used in this book.

Manufacturers of RFID hardware, particularly if they also manufacture both types of tags, are likely to provide readers that are capable of reading both ISO 15693 and ISO 18000-3 tags. However, because the two tags are not truly interoperable, such readers are configured to automatically alternate between trying to read one type of tag and trying to read the other. Performance of a reader in a mixed-tag environment is therefore impaired due to the time required to switch between reading modes.

While ISO 18000-3 establishes a standard for RFID, it is a general technology standard that addresses the air interface communication—how a tag and a reader communicate with each other. ISO 18000-3 establishes a "Reader Talks First" (RTF) protocol that defines how a reader accesses data programmed into a tag. With RTF communication, the reader sends a "wake-up" signal to the tag; only then does the tag respond. Among other things, the standard does not address the issue of how security should be handled in an RFID environment or if security should be included at all. Therefore, some ISO 18000-3 compliant tags that operate according to RTF for data retrieval have an embedded EAS bit that operates according to a "Tag Talks First" (TTF) protocol. See the section on materials security within an RFID environment in this chapter for more detailed information.

It is worth repeating that both ISO 15693 and ISO 18000-3 are technology standards, not application standards. While both are relevant for libraries, neither was designed specifically for libraries. In theory, this means that all tag and reader manufacturers who adhere to a common standard will be capable of reading each other's tags. However, in practice, this may not be the case. Please see the section titled *Data Structure, Capacity, and Content* later in this chapter for a full discussion of this topic.

3.1.2   Read/Write versus Write Once, Read Many Tags

Two types of RFID tags are used in libraries, read/write (R/W) and write once, read many (WORM). WORM tags allow information to be written to them only once. After the tag has been programmed, it cannot be changed or reprogrammed. Even turning on or off a single bit is not possible; this is a "writing" function. WORM tags do not have an EAS security bit (an indicator) that is set to "off" when an item is checked out and "on" when the item is checked in.

WORM tags often have a limited memory capacity, sufficient for holding an item's identification number but little more. Generally, the process of programming a WORM tag is slower and more complicated than that used for an R/W tag. However, a WORM tag is written to only once in its lifetime. Little energy is required to read a WORM tag. As a result, WORM tags can generally be read from 10 to 12 inches.

The R/W tags are available with various memory capacities. Vendors offer R/W tags with memory configurations ranging from 128 bits to a kilobit. In addition to the memory used for holding library-defined data, some R/W tags have a bit specifically designated for EAS purposes. Other R/W tags allow any bit in the tag's memory to be assigned the EAS function. In either case, it is this EAS function that is most central to an R/W tag. Library applications automatically turn the EAS bit off during check out and on during check in. Unlike WORM tags, other data may also be rewritten. However, most vendors recommend that the item identification (bar-code number) be "locked" to ensure that this mission-critical information is not accidentally changed. It is therefore important that R/W tags have separate memory fields (groupings of bits) that can be individually locked. This capability allows the item identification number to be locked without limiting the library's ability to change other information (genre, ownership information, location code, part number, etc.).

The R/W tag programming is usually quite simple and fast. In most cases, all that is required is scanning an item's existing bar code. Because R/W tags can be both read from and written to, and tag writing consumes more energy than reading, the range of R/W tags, around 6 inches, is less than that of WORM tags (10 to 12 inches).

The differences between WORM and R/W tags have significant ramifications for every aspect of an RFID system. They are addressed in detail in the sections of this book that discuss the individual applications of RFID.

3.1.3   Electronic Article Surveillance Capabilities

There are four approaches to the integration of materials security within an RFID system:

1.   Security system without RFID
2.   Server-based system utilizing item identification
3.   Reader Talk First (RTF) utilizing EAS security bit
4.   Tag Talk First (TTF) utilizing EAS security bit

Security system without RFID.

While most RFID systems provide the option of including materials loss-prevention security, the library may choose not to implement this functionality. Alternatively, a library can choose to use another EAS technology, such as electromagnetic (EM), for security purposes while using RFID for item identification. In all likelihood, only libraries with existing security systems would consider separating item identification from security functionality. Separating these functions forces the library to continue inserting security strips into materials as well as affixing RFID tags. Additionally, during discharging and charging operations, a separate step is required to deactivate (desensitize) and reactivate (resensitize) the EAS strips.

Using a different system for security purposes also eliminates the advantages that RFID presents during circulation transactions, such as the ability to process multiple items simultaneously without regard to orientation. In an EM environment, in order to minimize materials handling and make patron self check-out reasonably simple, bar-code labels must be attached to materials uniformly. This placement is necessary so that when an item's bar-code is placed under the bar code scanner, its security strip is automatically oriented in the correct position relative to the system's desensitizer. As a result, check out and security-strip desensitization can be done in a single step, either by a patron at a self check-out station or by staff members at a staff station. On the other hand, the benefit of RFID tags is that they can be read in any orientation and without a direct line-of-sight connection between tags and readers. If RFID and EM security are used together, nothing forces the user to correctly orient the security strips relative to the desensitizer. The likely result is that some (or many) materials will be checked out without desensitizing their security strips. Then, when the patron tries to exit the library, the security system is set off.

The additional complexity caused by using RFID and EM together also applies to automated returns and sorting systems. In order to check in and resensitize an item's security strip, exact item placement is required. Patrons' automated self-service returns become more difficult than need be. Furthermore, the cost of a system that can read RFID tags and resensitize security strips is substantially higher than a system that works solely with RFID technology. The alternative is to have staff resensitize security strips with a separate manual step after materials have been checked in automatically via RFID at an automated return.

Server-based system using item identification.

As noted earlier, a WORM tag does not have an EAS security bit that can be turned on and off. Security functionality in a WORM environment is accomplished only through database interrogation. WORM-based RFID security gates attempt to read the item identification numbers embedded within the tags and must send that data to a server in order to verify that the identified materials are checked out. When a match cannot be found, the server sends a message back to the security gates with an instruction to set off the alarm.

A server-based security system requires that the library's network and database be up and running properly in order to validate check out. System performance can vary based on the load on the server (servers used for security purposes may be dedicated or used for other tasks) as well as the number of tags that are within the reading field of the security gates. In the case of server overload, tags may be accurately read and recorded at the exit, but there is an unacceptable delay in the activation of the alarm. In the case of multiple tags to be read simultaneously, the sheer volume of information from WORM tags that the RFID gate readers must process instantaneously can have a deleterious effect on accurate tag detection. While reading the complete bar-code numbers for two or three tags is generally accomplished without difficulty, reading more than two or three tags can result in increasingly negative performance results. Note that WORM systems require RFID exit readers to interrogate all items within the field, those that have been successfully checked out as well as those that have not.

Reader Talk First utilizing EAS security bit.

As stated earlier, Read/Write tags usually incorporate a single bit that is used for EAS. That bit is automatically turned off when an item is checked out and turned on when an item is checked in. In an RTF security environment, security gates attempt to interrogate each tag as it enters the reading field created by the security pedestals in order to determine if the EAS bit is on or off. The detection of an "on" EAS bit creates a security "event" and the associated alarms—audio, visual, or both—are set off.

In one respect, RTF technology utilizing an EAS R/W security bit is similar to a server-based security system used in a WORM environment. Both systems use RFID readers at the building's exits that attempt to read data in the tags that are within the field created by the security pedestals. There are two important differences, however. First, while the server-based system used in a WORM environment requires that the entire bar-code number be read, the R/W EAS system requires only that a single bit be read. Second, once a WORM tag's number is read successfully, that data must be communicated to the server. The server must interrogate the item's ID number against the database, and only after the item's security status is determined to be "not checked out," is an alert sent back to the security gates. On the other hand, in an R/W EAS system, once an "on" bit is recognized, the alarms are sounded immediately. And, even if the library's server is off-line or there are network problems, security gates continue to operate normally.

The fact that both systems use RTF technology means that the detection capability for both suffers as the number of tags within the field increases. This makes sense when it is understood that when we speak of multiple RFID tags being read simultaneously, we are, in reality, referring to a process whereby each is read one right after the other, albeit very quickly. Security gate tag readers must read as many tags as there are in the field. When that number exceeds a handful, some tags will inevitably fail to be read. However, since the amount of information to be read in an R/W EAS bit environment is less than that of a server-based WORM environment, the performance degradation with multiple tag reading is not as severe. The graph below illustrates this point.

Tag Talk First utilizing EAS security bit.

As noted previously, ISO 18000-3 establishes RTF as the standard communications protocol. With RTF communication, the tag reader attempts to read the tags within the

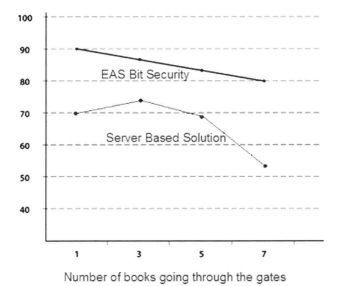

Figure 3.3. R/W EAS vs. server-based security performance.

interrogation zone; only then do the tags respond by returning their data to the reader. However, because the standard does not address materials security at all, ISO-compliant systems need not use RTF for security purposes. Therefore, some RFID vendors use RTF communications protocol for general tag reading during item circulation and shelf maintenance and use TTF protocol for security. In a TTF environment, all tags within the field created by the gates are "energized," but only those with "on" security bits send out a signal, often referred to as a "burst." Stated somewhat differently, the security gates detect only those bits that are "on." They do not attempt to read all tags as they would in an RTF environment. As a result, the detection performance of RFID security systems using TTF protocol does not deteriorate as the number of tags in the field increases. Tags are not waiting to be read; any tag with an active EAS bit will send a burst to the gate and set off the alarm. The graph below shows this consistent detection level compared to the other two approaches discussed earlier.

A Note Concerning Specific Item Identification at Security Gates: As we have explained, a server-based system is designed to capture the item IDs of those materials that have not been properly checked out. Most vendors offering R/W EAS bit solutions, either RTF- or TTF-based, can also provide item ID information on those items that set off the security gates as a standard or optional feature. It should be noted, however, that the R/W EAS bit-based security system's ability to accurately record item identification numbers does not measure up to its ability to recognize "on" security bits. Because the overall security bit detection capability of the TTF system is higher to begin with, this performance difference appears to be more pronounced. Therefore, should a library choose to implement item identification functionality, it should recognize that there are likely to be cases in which the exit sensors are alarmed but the item ID is not recorded.

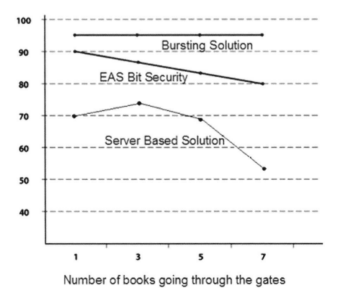

Figure 3.4. R/W EAS, bursting, and server-based security performance.

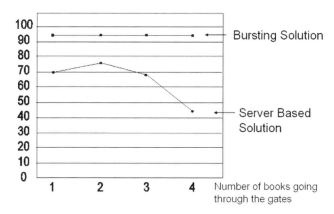

Figure 3.5. Bursting vs. server-based security performance.

3.1.4 Physical Construction

RFID tags are distinguishable from each other based on seven physical features: size and shape, the computer chip's "bump," the material from which the antenna is constructed, the bond between the chip and antenna, the substrate to which the chip and antenna are bonded, surface appearance (plain or imprinted), and the adhesive used to apply the tag to the item. Standard tags, as they are commonly referred to in libraries, are applied to print materials as well as to other library items, including audio books, video-cassettes, multimedia "bagged" materials, CD cases, and DVD cases. Most vendors also offer AV tags, sometimes referred to as "donut" tags that are applied directly to the inner hub of a disk. Tags designed specifically to be placed on the spine or under the flap of videocassettes are also available. These tags generally cost more than standard tags that can be applied to the face of a video. Moreover, at the time of this writing, many libraries are discarding their videocassette collections altogether.

Standard tag profile.

While most standard tags measure approximately 2 inches by 2 inches, some vendors offer tags that are significantly larger. The length of the antenna determines a tag's height and width. All other things being equal, the longer the antenna, the greater the read range. When the tag's antenna enters the electromagnetic field transmitted by an RFID reader, the antenna gathers the energy from the RF field and activates the chip. As a result of technological advances, the 2-inch-by-2-inch tags being manufactured today provide read ranges equivalent to those of tags manufactured just a few years ago that were twice as large. We anticipate that future advances will yield smaller and smaller tags with greater and greater read ranges. It is important to note that a greater read range is not necessarily better; the objective is to read only those tags designated for a particular application and no others that happen to be in or near the RF field. RFID readers commonly used in circulation and shelf-reading functions read the standard tags supplied to libraries today from a distance of 6 to 12 inches. As noted earlier, WORM tags may be read from greater distances than R/W tags. Readers used in security gates read these tags from a distance of 18 to 24 inches.

Tag antenna.

The antennae used in the manufacture of RFID tags used in libraries are made of metal, copper or aluminum. Libraries rightfully expect, and most vendors guarantee, that tags will live as long as the materials to which they are applied. Not surprisingly, the antenna material and the quality of its manufacturing process must be significantly superior to those used in tags that are designed for a limited life span. In an effort to drive down the cost of tags, manufacturers continue to seek out new materials and combinations of materials to use in making RFID antennae. At the current time, processes such as the use of conductive inks instead of metals hold great promise for limited life tags but are not suitable for the permanent tags needed in libraries.

Chip profile.

While the length of the antenna determines the height and width of the tag, it is the computer chip contained within the tag that should be examined carefully for the physical bump that it creates. The first generation of RFID tags for library systems had computer chips that were easily felt and seen. Technological advances now allow chips to be manufactured with a virtually unnoticeable bump. This makes the tag easier to disguise and reduces the likelihood that the chip will be damaged. RFID vendors can now supply libraries lower profile tags with memory sufficient to accomplish all required tasks.

Bond between chip and antenna.

Proper tag performance depends not only on the quality of the antenna and the chip but also on the physical connection between the two. Many manufacturers use what is called a "flip-chip" process to ensure that the bond between antenna and chip remains stable even through the rough handling of materials in book drops and sorting equipment.

Film and paper substrates.

The third component of an RFID tag is the substrate (the underlying layer) to which both the computer chip and antenna are bonded. While most tags use a paper substrate, films are also available from some vendors. The use of a film substrate adds a degree of durability to the tag but, generally, comes with a higher cost. Many libraries choose to place protective label shields over their tags. These can also be made from either paper or film.

Plain and imprinted tags.

While many libraries choose plain white tags, tags imprinted with text or graphics, usually the institution's logo, are also available. This imprinting disguises the tag's purpose and helps to conceal the antenna and chip that, especially in the case of paper tags, can show through. Most vendors offer custom imprinted tags and some provide equipment that prints on the tag at the same time when it is programmed. To date, however, the majority of libraries that have migrated to RFID technology have opted for plain RFID tags used together with preprinted protective labels, usually manufactured from vinyl or polyester film. While this does add an additional step to the conversion process, there are a number of advantages. The printing quality is generally superior than that found on vendor-supplied preprinted tags or tags printed by the library itself. The cover label provides the RFID tag with an additional layer of protection and thoroughly conceals the antenna and chip. And because labels are usually larger than the RFID tags, they help secure tags to library materials. Depending on the type of printing desired, the cost of a plain tag plus a protective label may actually be less than the cost of a preprinted tag.

RFID tags are self adhesive. While vendors promote their tags as being acid free and some may even refer to them as being of archival quality, libraries should treat RFID tags just as they would treat any other material that they would consider affixing to materials.

AV materials.

Other than physical dimensions, the issues discussed above relating to standard also apply to audiovisual (AV) tags. In the context of RFID, the term AV is used to refer to CDs and DVDs. While standard tags can be applied to CD jewel boxes or DVD cases, most vendors offer "donut" style tags that can be applied directly to the disks themselves. As the donut term implies, these tags have holes in their centers that are the size of the holes in the disks themselves. The entire tag is approximately one and a half inches in diameter, designed to fit into the inner hub of a disk, where, in many cases, no text or graphic appears and where a library may place its own label.

CDs and DVDs present special challenges for the RFID library. The metallic construction of the CD or DVD can interfere with or block the reading and writing of data from and to the RFID tags. In addition, the thin size of CDs and DVDs and the exact alignment of tags that often results when individual disks in multidisk sets are tagged directly can further compromise the read/write performance. Because CDs and DVDs are often at higher risk of theft than other items in a collection, some libraries choose to take additional steps to secure some or all of their CDs and DVDs. It should be noted, however, that many of the issues related to CD/DVD security apply to non-RFID libraries as well. From a security perspective, the approach that a library takes regarding the treatment of AV materials should be determined only after an analysis of two key questions: (1) How great is the risk of theft? and (2) How important are speed and ease of use during conversion and materials circulation processes? Most measures taken to prevent theft add time and complexity to the tagging process and/or circulation transactions. Finding a proper balance between the two, particularly during this time of rapid technological change, is one of the more difficult challenges libraries must meet in transitioning to RFID.

Let us further clarify specific problems in using RFID with CDs and DVDs. RFID signals easily travel through nonmetallic materials such as wood and plastic. RFID readers may therefore be mounted in or under desktops. Metal, on the other hand, can block or distort radio signals. When checking out materials in a traditional RF security system environment, RF security tags are "detuned" (deactivated) by date due cards, receipts, or labels that are impregnated with metal. What is true of RF systems in this regard holds equally true for RFID.

Current manufacturing processes encode content into a metallic-based material that covers plastic disks. This metal may block RFID transmissions if a substantial portion of the RFID tag is in direct or nearly direct contact with it. The circular donut tag is placed directly in the center hub position of the CD or DVD that normally does not contain metal. However, because metal-based inks are commonly used to imprint graphics on CDs and DVDs, this metal-free zone varies in size from disk to disk. In some cases, graphics cover the entire disk, from the outer edge all the way to the center hole. To further complicate matters, the nature and amount of metal used in these inks also may vary from one disk to another.

The only thing that can be said with certainty is that it cannot be said with certainty which disks are and are not proper candidates for RFID donut tags. Experience to date has shown that despite the metal construction of disks, the performance of these tags during charging and discharging processes is likely to be satisfactory, particularly if handled individually. But the same tag on the same disk that is read or written to without difficulty during check out or check in is not likely to perform adequately for security detection purposes. As noted earlier in our discussion about the different approaches to security within an RFID environment, the pick rate (the percentage of items correctly identified at security gates that are not properly checked out) varies based on the type of RFID system used. However, regardless of the system used, when only a few tags are present within the reading field of the security gates, the pick rate approaches and in some cases exceeds 90%. While this is true in the case of standard tags, the same cannot be said of AV tags where the pick rate, even when only one disk is present in the field, is likely to fall below 50%.

Based on the current state of RFID technology, it can be concluded that the AV donut works well in charging and discharging transactions when (1) only one item is processed at a time or multiple items to be processed simultaneously are spread out across the RFID reader and (2) only one disk in a multi-item set is tagged. It is difficult to generalize about multi-item sets since they vary both in terms of the number of disks in the case as well as their placement in the case. A two-disk set where both disks are tagged can work well since RFID readers create wraparound fields, like arms reaching out from both sides with hands that then join in the middle and are pulled back in toward the body.

Effectively this means that even though materials to be checked out are placed on top of the reader, the reader emits signals that communicate not only from below but also from above the materials. While the metal in the bottom disk may block signals coming directly from the RFID reader below it, the top disk would still be read by the wraparound signals that circumvent the bottom disk to reach the top disk from above. It can be easily understand why; when three or more disks are present in a set, the tags on disks at the top and the bottom may be read while the ones in the middle will not.

That said, the exact placement of individual disks within the case and the space between them may affect reading performance. In some cases, disks are aligned one directly on top of the other, while in others, they are staggered. Vertical spacing between disks, even just a millimeter, can make a significant difference. When combining these two factors with the differences that we have already discussed in the disks themselves, it is easy to realize how difficult it is to establish a uniform approach to the direct tagging of all disks in a library's collection.

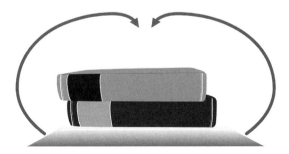

Figure 3.6. Wrap-around field.

Since even a single donut-tagged disk is likely to go undetected at security gates, the discussion above concerning multi-item sets is moot; their detection will be the same or worse. Libraries that are not overly concerned with theft may find this acceptable; such libraries may decide to forego the installation of security gates altogether. Libraries without serious loss-prevention concerns are therefore free to focus their attention on the other RFID functionalities and make their determination concerning the handling of AV materials accordingly. If AV theft is a serious problem, other measures for their protection should be considered.

AV booster antennae.

Some RFID vendors promote the use of "booster" tags or antennae to improve the reading of donut tags despite the metallic content of the disks to which they are applied. The first generation of boosters was designed to be placed in cases, not physically affixed to disks themselves. These boosters never gained acceptance in the marketplace due to doubts about their effectiveness from two perspectives. First, even if they did indeed boost the tags' signal strength, the boosters would provide no protection against thieves who choose to remove disks from their cases in order to exit without being detected. Second, tag reading was not demonstrably improved.

Vendors now offer boosters that can be affixed directly to the disks themselves. In some cases, these boosters are separate from the donut tags. Others are already integrated into the AV RFID tags. In either case, the booster covers the entire surface of the disk so that the RFID tag's antenna is extended to the outer edge of the disk. Those familiar with electromagnetic (EM) security systems, will find that the application of an RFID AV booster is similar to the EM CD security tag, in which the security strip is embedded into a clear circular film label that covers the disk. Both are self adhesive and require that care be taken to ensure exact placement and to make certain that the playing of the disk is unaffected.

At the time of this writing, the effectiveness of these self-adhering boosters has not been clearly demonstrated across a wide range of differently manufactured disks. It is not clear, in fact, whether they perform demonstrably better than the separate boosters placed in cases. Again, since most AV tags work reasonably well in non-security processes,

Figure 3.7. AV booster RFID tag.

subject to the limitations of multiple item processing and multidisk sets noted earlier, the measure of improved performance is determined by their detection at the exits. Libraries considering the use of boosters are advised to closely scrutinize vendor claims in this regard. Libraries must see for themselves whether the boosters markedly improve security detection in a real-world library environment. The extent of improvement should then be subjected to a cost-benefit analysis considering the price of the boosters, sometimes as much, if not more than the tags themselves, and the additional time that may be required to convert AV materials to RFID.

Multiple item reading and multi-item sets.

As noted earlier, once satisfied with the degree of loss-prevention protection offered, regardless of the criteria used to establish that level of satisfaction, a library can choose to turn its attention to circulation functionalities. Boosters may or may not effectively address the difficulties in tag reading that can be present when attempting to read multiple stacked AV items simultaneously or a multi-item set, particularly when three or more disks are present. The processing of multiple AV items can be accomplished either by handling each item individually or by spreading items out across the RFID reader to avoid the metal interference that may be created when items are stacked.

The challenges presented by multi-item sets cannot be similarly addressed. Libraries must weigh the potential benefits of tagging each disk in a set individually against tagging just one disk in the set or simply tagging the case itself. Skepticism has already been noted concerning potential security benefits, even when using boosters. However, even if boosters fail to produce a superior security environment, libraries can find benefit if each disk in a multidisk set can be individually recognized during check out, check in, and inventory without opening the case. For example, this would allow staff to determine whether all disks are present before checking in a multi-item set. Unfortunately, at this time, we cannot determine with a high degree of confidence whether the boosters currently offered by RFID vendors work well enough to allow their use for this purpose on multidisk sets.

If a library's own testing does not indicate that a strong majority of the individually tagged disks in multi-item sets are consistently read, with or without the aid of boosters, it will not be able to take advantage of the RFID benefit discussed above. A choice must be made between tagging just one disk in the set with an AV donut tag and tagging the case with a standard book tag. The advantages and disadvantages of both approaches are discussed in further detail in the section titled "Conversion" in this chapter.

3.1.5   Data Structure, Capacity, and Content

We began our discussion of tags by addressing the issue of standards and noting those that are relevant to libraries. It is worth noting again that the standards that do exist at the current time are general technology standards, not application standards. They address the air interface communication, in other words, how RFID tags and readers communicate with each other. There is no standard that addresses what information should be contained in a tag and how that information should be structured.

Data capacity.

Tags used in libraries today have data capacities, which range from 12 bytes (96 bits) to 256 bytes (2056 bits or 2 kilobits). WORM tags require only enough memory to hold item ID (bar code) numbers. Standard bar codes used in North American libraries consist of 14 digits, including what is referred to as the check digit, using the following typical format:

New England Public Library

3123412348

Figure 3.8. Library bar code.

Only 56 bits are needed to hold a 14-digit number which means that the 96-bit memory commonly used in WORM tags is more than sufficient to do the job. When converting to RFID, the bar-code format shown above is relevant only to the extent that the tag's data structure has an individual field that is a minimum of 64 bits in size. Some earlier generation tags that were not designed with North American libraries in mind did not contain sufficient memory in any single data field to accommodate an entire 14-digit number. Vendors took different approaches to deal with this limitation. Some broke the number up between different fields, placing the initial five digits, which remain constant for all materials in a library's collection, in one field and the remaining "variable" nine digits in a second field. Other vendors used a single "stand-in" digit in place of the starting five constant digits (materials code "3" and the four-digit library identification number). When the number is read, a lookup table built into the tag-reading software inserts the five constant digits in the place of the single stand-in digit. Both approaches worked and continue to work well. Tags manufactured today do not require either of these workarounds since individual field sizes are sufficient to hold all the required digits. This is just one example of how different vendors supplying libraries with identical tags may use data formats that are incompatible. Unless special steps are taken, these tags will not be able to both recognize and translate the data.

We said before that tags have a number of fields. There is, however, no inherent reason why a tag's memory need be broken up into various fields at all. A single field is all that is necessary when using WORM tags that only hold bar-code numbers and have no EAS security bit. The various R/W tags have a variety of possible memory sizes and configurations. Some vendors even offer tags with varying data capacities. For example, tag manufacturer Tagsys suggests that the memory of its ISO 18000-3 tag be divided as shown in the table below.

Tagsys also offers libraries an ISO 15693 tag with a kilobit (1024 bits) of memory. Some European countries have taken a lead in establishing standardized data structures. Ultimately, the objective is to allow for tagging at the source, built into the actual construction of the materials so that the tag's presence is totally concealed. Whether this approach is likely to gain quick acceptance in North America remains to be seen, particularly given the tremendous diversity of publishers that exist here. The publishing industries in those countries that are moving in the direction of fixed standards for tag memory, such as Denmark and the Netherlands, are already standardized to a much greater degree than in North America. As such, adding another standard for RFID does not present as great a challenge as it does here. Nonetheless, the standardization

Table 3.2. Tagsys 320 Data Structure

Block/ Function	Access	Fields	Size	Required/ Optional	Used for
Block 1 Real-Time Data	Locked	Bar code (14 numeric digits)	56 bits	Required	Compatibility with bar code systems
		Reference item	1 bit	Optional (recommended)	Keeps reference materials from leaving the library.
		Pre-Sorted data	3 bits	Optional (recommended)	Fast sorting at return
		Item type	4 bits	Optinal (recommended)	Use same ID for patrons and items. Fast detection
Block 2 Item Data	Read/ Write	Check In/Out status (date, operation)	32 bits	Optional (recommended)	Fast detection at Item inventory. Operation Proof.
		Multi-item identification	16 bits	Optional (recommended)	Sub-item identification
		Shelving section	16 bits	Optional (recommended)	Fast sorting at return
Block 3 Library Data	Locked	Library Identifier	32 bits	Optional	For inter-library loans, identifies library
		Branch Identifier	32 bits	Optional	Identifies a branch within a library system
Block 4 User-Defined	Locked or read/ write defined)	Library-specific custom data	64 bits	Optional	Allows the library to define any custom information to store

experiences of these countries should be monitored closely for potential applicability in North America. See Chapter 2 for more information on the RFID data structure recommended in Denmark in July 2005.

To the extent that more than just the bar code is programmed into the tag, breaking up the data into multiple fields allows each piece of information to be individually locked. As implied, once initially programmed, locked data cannot be changed. Locked fields prevent the possibility that when programming one tag, another tag in the vicinity could inadvertently be programmed. For this reason, it is advisable to lock the "mission-critical" bar-code number. Other information that a library chooses to include in the tag is not likely to fall into the mission-critical category. When information is likely to be changed, it should be placed in a nonlocked field.

Data content.

RFID tags can potentially hold significant volumes of data above and beyond the basic bar-code number. This includes, but is not limited to, bibliographic information (author, title, subject), ownership information, shelving location, item type, circulation status (circulating or non circulating), and multipart set information. A more detailed discussion on data content can be found in Chapter 2, including specifics concerning the Danish library model. For our purposes here, it is sufficient to note that the only data that will be found in all RFID tags is the item identification or bar-code number. However, as noted earlier, even that information can be encoded differently from vendor to vendor. Suffice it to say that there is no official standard or de facto standard for what data to include in a tag and how that data should be formatted.

While there are no standards concerning data content, the American Library Association has issued guidelines directed toward the protection of patron privacy (American Library Association, 2005). Those guidelines can be summarized as follows: less is more—less information affords greater privacy protection. Although the Danish RFID Data Model for Libraries recommends 32-byte tags, memories significantly smaller are sufficient to hold the mission-critical bar-code number. Vendors promoting tags with larger memories, some as large as 2 kilobits, do not offer specific recommendations as to how all this excess memory should be used. Rather, they encourage prospective libraries to believe that this memory may be useful at some point in the future.

A general note concerning tag quality: The manufacturing process for RFID tags is a complex one; a certain rate of errors is to be expected. The error percentage should not exceed 2%, and as a matter of standard manufacturing policy, manufacturers should include extra tags on each roll to compensate. RFID and wireless technologies can easily interfere with one another, and untold numbers of devices involving whirling metal can produce radio waves at many frequencies. Debugging these types of problems is difficult and requires many different skills (Heinrich, 2005). An RFID tag can be expected to have a life span of approximately 100,000 cycles. Since each read uses 15 to 20 cycles (Chachra, 2005), this means that each tag can be read approximately 5,000 to 6,667 times.

Libraries are advised to purchase tags from reputable vendors who specialize in the manufacture of tags specifically for library applications and are active in promoting the evolving RFID standards. RFID technology is quickly gaining acceptance in many industries, providing a wide variety of functionalities. As a result, different tag construction processes are being explored that should both improve performance and lower prices. Tag builders are researching not only the use of different materials but also the manufacturing process itself, such as using printed circuitry as opposed to using a metal or similar substrate. Do not, however, assume all processes are appropriate for tags used in a library.

3.2 READERS

A data capture device is called a reader, regardless of whether it only reads data or is also capable of writing data (Finkenzeller, 2003). It may also be called a transceiver or, when separated from its antenna, a coupler. The reader manages radio communication with a tag through the RFID application software. Passive tags used in libraries respond to activation and commands from the reader. Unlike active tags used in some nonlibrary environments, passive tags never emit signals independently (Finkenzeller, 2003). Rather, the RFID application software residing on the computer attached to the reader extracts the required data for the specific function being used. Depending on the function, it may pass that data to the appropriate ILS application. The "dumb" readers described above only read tags and send data to a central collection point, which filters and smoothes the data for analysis. That said, as the technology further develops, "dumb" readers may be replaced by more highly functional "smart" RFID readers that can perform intelligent

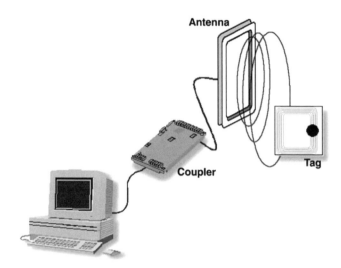

Figure 3.9. Tag reader, coupler, and antenna.

operations beyond simple communication (Sweeney, 2005). While some RFID vendors recommend data encryption, currently, that functionality, if provided, is performed by the application software that resides on the computer and not by the readers themselves. If data encryption gains wider acceptance in the marketplace, it is logical to expect that this capability, together with data authentication functionalities, will be built into readers.

The reader is powered from a wall outlet, a heavy-duty battery, or, in some cases, a laptop computer. The flow of electricity to an antenna is controlled by the complex circuitry anchored by the Digital Signal Processor (DSP) (Sweeney, 2005). Antennae can be set up to be continuously active or to activate upon command. The continuously active mode is used primarily at protected exits, although some security gates, in the interest of preventing false alarms, are activated through physical sensors.

There are two fundamental components of a reader: a control unit and a high frequency (HF) interface. The HF interface consists of a transmitting antenna and a receiving antenna, though many readers use the same antenna for both transmitting and receiving signals (Finkenzeller, 2003). The HF interface generates high frequency transmission power, which activates the tag, supplies it with power, transmits signals, and receives data in return.

The electromagnetic wave emitted by an RFID reader is scattered in many directions throughout the air. This electromagnetic wave reaches a tag's antenna that reflects part of the wave back to the reader's antenna. As the distance from the radiation source increases, the size of reflected wave decreases. An inverse relationship also exists between data transit speed and the read range. Higher transmission speeds accompany lower read ranges, usually of just few inches. Other than at security gates, read ranges are measured in inches as opposed to feet.

3.2.1　Types of Readers

Different types of readers are designed for specific purposes. A standard library "fixed-location" circulation application generally utilizes a reader comprised of a pad-type

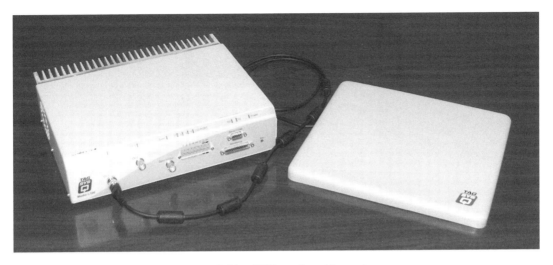

Figure 3.10. RFID reader with coupler.

antenna that is connected to a coupler. The brains of the operation, so to speak, are controlled through firmware, software that is embedded in the device. These types of readers are like earlier generation bar-code scanning systems, many of which are still being sold and used today. Those systems consist of a scanning device (a light pen or a laser scanner, for example) that connects to a computer through a "wedge." The pad antenna is analogous to the scanning device while the coupler is analogous to the wedge.

Some lower-powered RFID readers have couplers that are built into the housing of the pad antenna. These readers are appropriate for the processing of one item at a time,

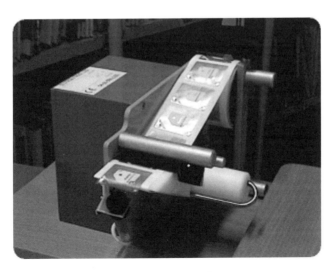

Figure 3.11. Program dispenser.

Figure 3.12. Handheld reader.

such as tag programming. Other applications may have couplers built into the antenna housing or connected externally. These include

- Tag programming dispensers (sometimes combined with printers)
- Security pedestals
- Hand-held readers

In addition to their functional objectives, readers should be compared and contrasted based on a number of other criteria:

- FCC Certification
- Read speed
- Read range
- Read accuracy
- Ability to read multiple tag protocols
- Physical footprint

FCC certification.

All readers should have FCC Part 15 Certification. FCC registrations can be found on its Web site at: https://gullfoss2.fcc.gov/prod/oet/cf/eas/reports/GenericSearch.cfm.

Libraries may also want to request that vendors supply their latest certifications concerning electromagnetic emissions.

Read speed.

It is important to emphasize that while it is common to speak of multiple RFID tags being read simultaneously, in reality, tags are read so rapidly, one after the other, that it appears they are read simultaneously. The actual speed of data transmission varies depending on its direction. Typical read speeds in a high speed ISO 18000-3, Mode 2 library environment are 26 kilobits per second (kbps) from reader to label and 52 kbps from label to reader. Read speed is a function not only of the reader but also of the tags. Tags that do not comply with the ISO 18000-3, Mode 2 standard may not read as quickly as those that do. Write speeds will usually be slower than read speeds. When checking out a book in a Read/Write RFID security environment, the process of turning off an EAS bit can take slightly longer than that required to read the item identification from the tag. However, the writing of multiple tags is indeed a simultaneous process since all tags in the fields are written to identically (RFID readers cannot isolate particular tags within a group for unique writing).

Not only can multiple RFID tags be read simultaneously, but they can also be read while the tag or reader is in motion. Tags can be read as they move across readers in security gates, in staff or patron self check-out stations, or in conveyor-belt sorting systems. It is the reader that moves across shelves when performing stack-maintenance activities such as taking inventory or searching for missing items.

In most situations, writing of RFID tags cannot be done reliably while tags are in motion. Therefore, only in WORM environments should staff or patrons wave items across RFID readers during check out and check in. In R/W systems, items should remain stationary until a signal is given that all items have been successfully processed.

Read range.

With the exception of security gates, RFID readers are limited in range to approximately 6 inches in R/W systems and 12 inches in WORM systems. It is important to note that more is not necessarily better when it comes to read range. Proper operation of an RFID system depends upon reading those tags that should be read during any particular application and not reading tags that may be close to but outside the designated read area. Libraries would create havoc if, during check out, items were mistakenly charged to a patron's account by virtue of the fact that they were in the vicinity of an RFID reader. Similarly, when performing shelf-reading tasks, it is not desirable to have a range so large that the reader picks up items that are on the shelf below or above, or on the opposite side of a double-faced unit.

Because of the proximity factor, libraries investigating RFID systems should closely examine how well prospective systems control and limit reading fields. As noted previously, signals emitted by RFID readers are not vertical; they do not extend in a straight line directly from the reader. Signals may extend horizontally beyond the physical borders of the reader itself, even moving up and around items that are on top of the reader. Read range and direction is dependent on a number of factors including the type of system used (WORM or R/W), and the power and construction of the reader. For example, a reader used for tag programming may purposefully have limited power that is focused in the center of the antenna. Greater power is not needed since the programming of tags is a one-at-a-time process. This limited and tightly focused reading range also ensures that tags close to the reader are not accidentally programmed with the same information as that of the tag being processed.

In some systems, the write range is less than the read range. Therefore, care should be taken to limit the number of items or the height of stacks that are being processed simultaneously to the write range of the system. This prevents items from being checked out or in without their security bits being changed accordingly.

Readers are available with special coatings, such as ferrite, that prevent signals from "bleeding" into unintended areas. In addition to avoiding the unintentional reading of tags, bleed control also limits the possibility of reader collision, a phenomenon that occurs when the operation of one reader interferes with that of another. Readers manufactured in this way can operate in relatively close proximity to one another, so that staff or self-service stations need not be separated any more than they would be in a non-RFID environment. A reader should be finely tuned to maximize its capability as this too prevents RF bleed from affecting adjacent systems (Sweeney, 2005).

RFID security pedestals must be able to read tags from much greater distances. All RFID security systems are designed to create aisles of at least 3 feet in width with some as wide as 4 feet. Most RFID security pedestals are bidirectional—that is, they emit a signal to both sides. That means, for instance, that a single pedestal can read tags up to 18 inches to its left and 18 inches to its right. At the same time, the system is likely to detect tags both in front of and behind the aisle that is created between two pedestals. The extended read range of security gates, particularly if not tightly confined, may result in the detection of extraneous RFID signals. To prevent the false alarms that could result, some manufacturers install sensors into the security pedestals that detect movement within the exit aisle. The reader activates only in response to a message from the sensors indicating that there is a person present between the gates.

Read accuracy.

The state of RFID technology has developed to the point where it is virtually certain that if a tag is read, it will be read correctly. Accuracy in an RFID context is therefore focused on reading all of the many tags that may be present within the target field. RFID systems have anticollision functionality to prevent the reading of one tag from interfering with another. This capability is usually measured in terms of the speed of anticollision reads, with 50 per second being a generally recognized standard. Despite the best efforts of manufacturers, application developers must be cognizant of the possibility of tag collision and make sure that measures are built into applications to recognize when it occurs. In this book, these measures are discussed in detail in the sections dealing with each application.

Ability to read multiple tag protocols.

In our discussion of tags, we explored the issue of RFID tags being read by equipment manufactured by different companies. In that discussion, which included an exploration of the relevant standards for libraries, we concluded that at the current time, it is unwise to make any decision based on claims of a vendor that the vendor's tags can be read by any reader. Despite the existence of communication standards, the absence of standards for security, data size, and data structure makes the kind of interoperability associated with bar codes absent when it comes to RFID. While the question of reader interoperability should be viewed with the same skepticism as tag interoperability, companies that manufacture readers to communicate with ISO standard tags should be able to program those readers to properly parse and decipher the data transmitted. In some cases, however, that may be possible only with cooperation of the company that originally supplied the library with its RFID system. However, just because a reader can be programmed to read multiple tag types does not mean that it will read all of them with the same speed or accuracy. Proper synchronization between the reader's and the tag's

Figure 3.13. RFID reader mounted under a desk.

timing devices is also required to guarantee optimal performance. Therefore, best results are ensured when tags and readers are purchased as a matched set.

Physical footprint.

The relevant footprints for security gates, tag programming/printing/dispensing units, hand-held shelf devices, self check-out, automated check in, and sorting equipment are defined by the physical structures of the components as supplied by the RFID vendor. Readers used by staff may be integrated in various ways into the library work environment. RFID antennae may be mounted in or under desks. Various lengths and widths of antennae are available to meet a variety of space constraints. Pad antennae are generally less than an inch thick with many as thin as a half inch. It is therefore important for RFID vendors to work closely with any designers that the library employs to ensure a proper fit.

3.2.2 Conversion Stations

In this section we address various hardware and software components that can be used to convert a library's collection to RFID. (For more depth on the project-management aspects of conversion, refer to Chapter 5.)

Conversion basics.

At the most basic level, RFID conversion means programming materials' item identification numbers into RFID tags. Given the developed state of library automation in North America, we begin with the premise that these identification numbers are contained within each item's bar code. Item identification numbers may therefore be referred to interchangeably as bar-code numbers. While that basic identification number is all that can be contained in standard library bar-code labels, RFID tags have the capacity to hold additional information as well. (Deciding what data to include in the tag is discussed in Chapters 2 and 5.)

Scanning an item's existing bar code is all that is necessary to program the item ID number into the tag and activate the tag's security bit. Some vendors' tags come with security bits already in the on position. Most systems allow the operator to visually verify the number on screen against the bar-code number on the book before writing

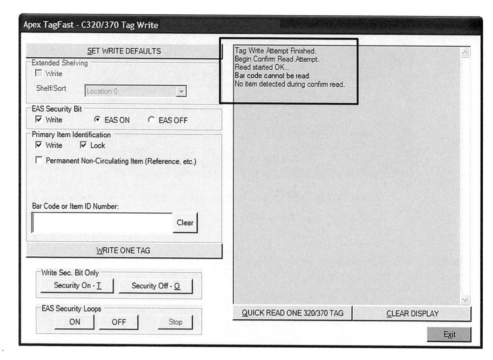

Figure 3.14.   Bar code unable to be read.

that information to the tag. However, the reliability of today's bar-code scanners makes this time-consuming step unnecessary. If the scanner picks up all digits, it will pick them up correctly. However, depending on the scanner being used or the condition of the bar-code label, a truncated read is possible. If the programming application includes a utility that verifies that all digits are present before writing the number to the RFID tag, the library should feel comfortable allowing the process to proceed automatically without visual inspection. For example, if bar-code numbers consist of 14 digits, when the bar-code scanner reads fewer than 14 digits, the application is interrupted, the RFID tag is not written to and the operator is notified.

If desired, sorting information (branch ownership and shelving area), item-type information (e.g., "reference"), and multipart set information may also be written to the tag. Because the conversion process is usually done on a section-by-section basis, sorting and item-type information need not be changed for each individual item since that information will be the same for all items in any particular section. The tag-programming application provided by the library's RFID vendor should allow for this information to be entered directly without need to interface with the item's bibliographic record in the ILS database. Therefore, no network connection is needed. A network connection to the library ILS should be required only if bibliographic information is programmed into the tag. Should the tag-programming application require access to the library's bibliographic database, it will likely do so through SIP2 or NCIP as provided by the ILS vendor.

The transition to RFID is often an ideal time to weed the library's collection. It is particularly advantageous if the library's ILS can create a file of all items that have not circulated over a designated period of time. Many RFID vendors allow for the uploading of that file into the tag-programming application. The file is interrogated before the tag is

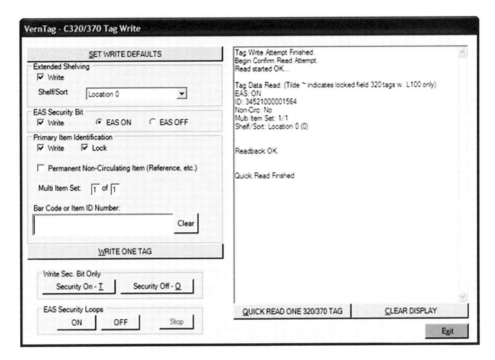

Figure 3.15. Tag programming application.

written. If the bar-code number of an item scanned matches a bar code on file, the opera-tor is notified. The operator can decide whether to proceed with the tag programming or pull the selection. If collection weeding is performed concurrently with the conversion process, tags should not be applied to materials until after they are programmed.

Depending on the conversion process workflow, a library that is not weeding at the same time may prefer to place an RFID tag in the book prior to programming. In order to do that, a pad-type RFID reader is needed. It is always best to program CD and DVD donut tags before applying them to disks.

Some vendors offer mobile conversion stations for purchase or lease that include all necessary components, including a heavy-duty battery to power the computer, a reader, and possibly a tag dispenser or printer. Alternatively, the library may choose to place a computer workstation or laptop on a mobile cart that may be wheeled through the aisles.

Programming data on RFID tags requires an RFID reader, a bar-code scanner, a com-puter, and application software. Some vendors offer devices that combine the reader, scanner, and computer into a single unit. In addition, some readers are equipped with label-dispensing functionality and/or printing functionality. The actual reader used will determine, to a great degree, the procedure used in tagging materials.

Hardware options.

RFID hardware options for tag programming include

- Standard staff station readers (couplers separate from pad antennae)
- Low-powered pad readers with built-in couplers designed specifically for tag programming

Figure 3.16. Mobile programming station.

- Tag programming/dispensers
- Tag programming/dispensers/printers

The next sections detail each of these options.

Standard staff stations. Along with materials circulation functionality, the ability to program tags is often included with standard staff stations. Since these stations are designed to expedite material check out and check in, they can read multiple items simultaneously. And because readers, upon instruction, write information to all tags that are present within the reading zone, care must be taken to ensure that only the specific tag designated for programming is in that zone. Other tags, particularly those that are not yet programmed, are still in their packaging, or on rolls, should be kept sufficiently clear of the zone. When applying tags to items before programming, a pad reader is particularly well suited. Staff apply the tags, place single items on the antenna, and scan the bar code. This latter technique works well with most print materials with the exception of those that have metallic imprinted covers (Chapter 5 provides suggested work-arounds for such materials). Additionally, the donut-style CD/DVD hub tags should be processed prior to placing them on disks. If the library wants to program tags before applying them to materials, programming/dispensing equipment is preferred. A programmer/dispenser is particularly useful when doing the initial collection conversion. We will discuss these programmer/dispensers in detail later in this section. If, for whatever reason, a pad reader is used when programming prior to physical application, two techniques are possible. The first technique frees both the operator's hands for the purpose of scanning the item bar code. The tag, still attached to its paper backing, is cut from the roll and placed directly on the pad reader. After it is programmed, the tag is pulled from its backing and placed on the item. The second option uses a one-handed scanning technique. In this process, the operator pulls the tag away from the roll and holds it by one edge over the reader at the same time that the bar code is scanned. The person using the scanner must take care to keep the tag far enough from the reader so that the tag's adhesive does not make contact with it.

Standard staff station readers require more power than can be delivered through a computer. They must be plugged into a wall outlet or, if used in the stacks, on a mobile cart, powered by an electrical extension cord plugged into the wall or a heavy-duty battery.

Low-powered pad readers with built-in couplers. Low-powered pad readers are designed specifically by RFID manufacturers for the purpose of programming tags. Some RFID vendors also incorporate staff circulation functionality into the software that works with these readers. However, when programming tags from staff stations that include this type of reader, libraries should limit their use to reading one item at a time. The process of programming tags with a low-powered reader is the same as described above with a standard staff station. However, the smaller RFID field created by the low-powered reader is not as likely to bleed to other tags that may be in the general vicinity. The risk of inadvertently programming tags other than the target tag is reduced. This reader can operate by power delivered from the computer that it is attached to; no battery or extension cord is needed.

Tag programmer/dispensers. In addition to programming tags, a programmer/dispenser separates the self-adhesive label from its paper backing so that the operator can pull the label away and place it on an item with one hand. The physical step of pulling the RFID tag off the roll is eliminated. The use of a programmer/dispenser is particularly advantageous when the library wants to program tags before placing them on items; the clumsy handling of single self-adhesive tags with a pad reader is eliminated.

Tag programmer/dispenser/printers. Some RFID vendors offer tag programmer/dispensers that are also capable of printing at the same time. This is advantageous for new items, not during conversion of the existing collection. In addition to standard text and logo, libraries can print the item's bar-code label and accompanying "eye-readable" number on the tag. Libraries may find it easier and less expensive to purchase either preprinted tags or imprinted protective label shields from their RFID vendors. The advantages and disadvantages to these different approaches are discussed in Chapter 5.

3.2.3 Staff Circulation Stations

In this section, we address RFID applications that are designed to allow staff to check out and check in library materials. While at least one RFID company has historically provided a single station for use by both patrons and staff, most vendors, recognizing the different needs and demands of each group, have created separate applications. We discuss the objectives and ramifications of a combined station in the self check-out section, directing our attention here to utilities used by staff only.

The process of checking in library materials shares much in common with that of checking out materials; where not specifically noted, assume that they are essentially identical, albeit in reverse. There are, however, a number of distinctions that require understanding so that appropriate workflow procedures may be instituted. Additionally, special attention need be given to stations that are used for both check out and check in—their functionality can switch back and forth multiple times throughout the day.

Staff check out.

A central question that every library must address, regardless of the technological environment, is "How many staff stations do we need?" The answer may vary according to many factors, some of which are *hard*, such as logistical and technological infrastructure, while others are *soft*, such as human and philosophical. Our objective here is to help the reader understand the possible approaches that will help the library successfully address the questions of how many stations to install, and where and how to install them.

From a hardware perspective, a staff station equipped with RFID functionality looks quite similar to a station dedicated to bar-code-scanning capabilities. To upgrade such a station to RFID, a library has to add only an RFID reader to the existing equipment. If desired, the reader can be hidden out of sight. RFID couplers can be stored under circulation desks next to computers in well-ventilated areas. Since RFID pad antennae can read through any nonmetallic object, they may be mounted beneath most library desktops with only a marginal decrease in range. Because they have a small physical footprint, measuring usually only about a half inch thick, most pads fit into existing desktop space without difficulty.

While RFID vendors are prepared to provide complete staff station solutions, most provide the ability to connect an RFID reader to and install RFID software on a library-supplied computer where the ILS circulation software already operates. With most RFID systems, the presence of an RFID reader has no effect on an existing bar-code scanner or receipt printer.

As is necessary in a bar-code-only environment, the check-out process begins with patron authentication. While RFID patron cards are available, they are costly, provide little benefit, and raise privacy concerns. As a result, few libraries have opted to replace their existing ba-coded patron cards with RFID cards. Patrons continue to present their cards to a staff person who scans them with a bar-code scanner. After a patron's borrowing privileges are approved by the ILS, the patron can begin checking out library materials.

RFID technology changes the process significantly. Individual item bar-code labels need not be located and individually scanned. First, with RFID, it makes no difference how an item is oriented and placed on the reader—cover up, cover down, spine in, spine out. As long as the item's tag is in the reading zone, it will be recognized. Second, in most RFID systems, a stack or stacks of materials can be processed at a staff station simultaneously. The library can instruct patrons to place all the items to be borrowed on the pad reader, or on a designated area on or above the RFID antenna. Staff need not touch materials at all, except to handle exceptions.

RFID technology can make the life of a circulation clerk much easier; it does not, however, eliminate a clerk's responsibilities altogether. In addition to handling all those things that have no relationship to RFID such as taking payment for fines, staff must be careful to note that all items placed on the RFID reader have been read. Inevitably, despite the library's best efforts, some items will not be tagged, particularly when the system first goes live. There may also be tag collision or tags that are simply outside the reader's range. Some systems provide a counter indicating how many tags the reader has successfully read. But one way or the other, staff must verify that all items have been processed. It is important to keep in mind that we are discussing staff stations, not self check-out stations. The library should be able to rely on trained staff persons to check whether all items are processed correctly. On the other hand, self check-out stations should be designed for the totally uninitiated user.

While the RFID hardware supplied by one vendor may look like and even operate in a very similar fashion to that supplied by another, the application software approaches may differ significantly. Most basic is the interface with the library's ILS. Some RFID staff applications communicate with the library's database through a third-party protocol, usually SIP2. Others insert bar-code numbers read from RFID tags directly into the item identification field of the ILS circulation screen. Still others offer individual staff the option of using either one of the approaches, even switching between them with the click of a mouse.

SIP-Based Applications. SIP-based applications require a SIP interface at staff stations, a feature that would probably not have been installed prior to using RFID. Depending on the library's contract with its ILS vendor, who would also supply a SIP license, there may or may not be cost implications. Libraries are advised to consult their ILS vendors before moving forward with any application, RFID related or not, that requires a SIP license. While systems that direct data into the library's native ILS client screen operate behind the scenes, SIP-based systems place the RFID application at the core of the check-out operation; staff work with the RFID vendor-supplied software as opposed to the native ILS circulation software. The RFID software cannot be said to be better or worse than the native ILS software. That will depend not only on the actual features of the two systems being compared but also on the operator. One staff person may find the RFID application easier to use than the ILS circulation software, while another will find the exact opposite to be true.

What can be said with certainty is that the SIP-based RFID application must be closed or minimized whenever staff need to access the ILS for non-RFID utilities. If, for example, an individual wishing to check out materials has an expired library card, the staff person needs to leave the RFID application and open the appropriate ILS module in order to update patron information. Some RFID systems can automatically copy the patron number for pasting into the proper field of the ILS, thereby eliminating at least one of the additional required steps.

Why would an RFID vendor go through the trouble of creating a separate interface when it is possible to allow staff to continue using the ILS application with which they are already familiar and comfortable? There are four reasons. First, in addition to reading the bar-code number, the RFID system must turn off the EAS security bit on R/W tags. Second, ILS circulation applications are designed to accept only one number at a time, not multiple numbers at a rapid fire pace. Third, there are functionalities of RFID systems that, if used, the native ILS circulation utility simply cannot handle. Finally, the development of a behind-the-scenes application that directs input to the proper field on the ILS screen may actually be more difficult and complex than that required for a SIP environment. Some further explanation will clarify these issues, not only in the context of a staff station but also as they relate to the entire nature of the communications interface between the RFID system and the library's ILS.

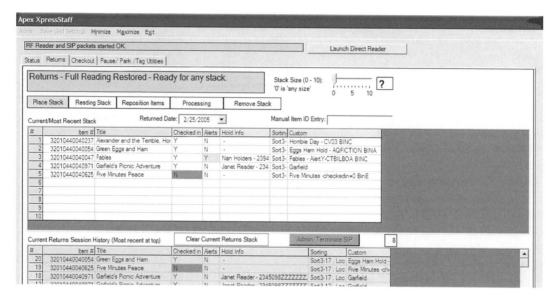

Figure 3.17. Staff circulation application with RFID.

Turning Off the EAS Security Bit. When checking out an item in a non-RFID library using a security system, a staff person scans the bar code and then, following approval from the ILS, does whatever is necessary to deactivate the security strip or tag. Materials with EM security strips must be passed across a desensitizer. Traditional RF security signals are most commonly blocked by placing special date due detuning cards in the book pockets that conceal the RF tags. In both cases, in addition to scanning the bar-code label, staff must perform a separate security-related task. In an RFID environment, the security function is handled automatically without any additional steps on the part of staff. This presents little challenge in an RFID WORM system since there is no security bit that needs to be turned off; the item's ID is recorded in a database and compared to the IDs of materials passing through security gates. From this perspective, RFID WORM systems work just like bar-code-based systems, the only differences being that RFID tags and readers are used instead of bar-code labels and scanners.

It is clearly desirable to streamline the check-out process as much as possible. To limit the number of steps taken and physical handling of materials to an absolute minimum, the check-out application of an RFID R/W system should turn off EAS bits without any additional action. If the EAS bit is to be turned off only after an item has been approved for check out, just as it would at a patron self-service station, the turnoff function is forced to be through SIP communication. However, as we noted earlier, it makes little sense to treat trained staff in the same way that you would an uninitiated patron. Some steps that are needed to ensure the integrity of a self check-out process are unnecessary at a staff station. And wherever a step can be eliminated without negative consequences, it should be. For example, an RFID staff station should turn off security bits without having to wait for check-out approval from the database. This assumes that upon receiving feedback from the ILS an item cannot be borrowed and that staff will prevent that item from accompanying the patron out of the library.

Reading Multiple Items. ILS circulation applications have a single field that accepts the item's bar-code number. That field is not designed to handle the streaming of multiple numbers that result from reading a stack of RFID-tagged materials. In addition, each RFID-tagged item has the potential of generating an exception comment or instruction to the operator. Most RFID vendors who allow the processing of multiple items simultaneously have found the challenge of managing this scenario to be impossible without using their own circulation applications, which communicate with the database through SIP. This challenge presents itself not only to vendors of R/W systems but also to vendors of WORM systems. If all materials brought to the circulation desk could be checked out without exception with no special instructions to staff, the processing of multiple items simultaneously could be handled with relative ease through the buffering of data input. However, the real world of today's library consists of many exceptions and special instructions. As a result, despite the misgivings that exist among librarians toward SIP and toward using any staff applications other than their native ILS application, most RFID vendors have chosen SIP-based staff stations that operate their own circulation software to be the easiest way to process multiple items simultaneously.

RFID-Specific Features. ILS circulation modules are not designed to accommodate all the features that libraries may want to incorporate once they have migrated from bar codes to RFID tags. These advanced features become possible when the vendor includes additional data in the tag, above and beyond the bar-code number. The handling of multipart sets is one example. If each individual part of a set has its own RFID tag, RFID-specific circulation software can transmit to the ILS, only after verifying that all parts are present and accounted for, the common bar-code number that is recognized by the ILS.

Difficulties of Direct Interface with ILS Systems. Even if the library chooses not to utilize RFID-specific functionality such as the multipart set utility described above, the challenge of turning off the security bit and correctly processing multiple items simultaneously remains. Vendors who have developed effective, direct RFID to ILS applications have done so by recognizing the often problematic real-world environment of a library circulation desk.

Direct RFID to ILS Interface. As discussed, the key obstacles to interfacing directly with native ILS circulation software without communication through SIP are turning off security bits and processing multiple items simultaneously. At least one vendor has found a way to successfully do both with only a minor caveat: security bits are turned off at the same time as tags are read and before items have been checked out in the ILS. Should a message come back from the ILS saying that check out for a specific item is not allowed, staff need to pull that item from the stack and, upon completion of the transaction, turn the security bit back on. This can be done quickly and easily with only a couple of mouse clicks. Hopefully, staff recognize reference and other materials that never circulate through cursory visual inspection so that they can be removed from the RFID reading zone before processing commences. The advantage of keeping the native ILS software on screen and operating at all times outweighs this relatively minor and hopefully infrequent inconvenience. The staff RFID circulation software that makes this possible operates behind the scenes and remains minimized unless some configuration change is required.

Staff check in.

With a few exceptions, everything in our discussion pertaining to staff check out applies to staff check in as well. The procedural differences between bar code and RFID functionality for check out also exist here. The introduction of RFID technology has unique implications regarding treatment of multipart sets and sorting which facilitates the quick return of materials to their proper locations in the library. These elements, together with a subtle, but important, difference in how staff verify that all items in a stack have been read, potentially give a SIP-based check-in approach, an advantage over a direct RFID to ILS approach.

While libraries may or may not check to see whether all parts of multipart sets are present when materials are checked out, most do check when materials are returned. If each part of a set is individually tagged, software provided by the RFID vendor may potentially be capable of determining whether all parts are present without having to open the case. First, we say *potentially* because it should not be automatically assumed that all RFID systems have this functionality. And second, the inherent difficulties of reading and writing to the donuts that are applied directly to CDs and DVDs (as described in the section on tags) are magnified when multiple disks are aligned one on top of the other. If this is determined not to be a problem of significant proportions and/or if the library is prepared to accept a certain percentage of "false negatives," multipart tagging may expedite the returns process significantly. In this context, a "false negative" occurs when the system reports that not all items are present even when they are. In such a case, staff would still need to open the case to check. There are, however, no "false positives." All items must be present in order for the RFID to detect them.

The ability of RFID to read multiple items simultaneously may not be of value if materials check in is combined with sorting which must be done on an item-by-item basis. A library may choose to program sorting locations into its RFID tags, using this

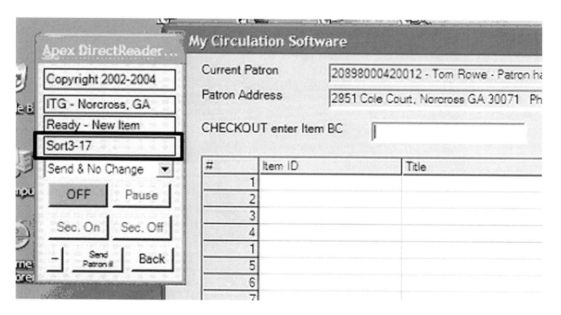

Figure 3.18. Example of locations stored on the RFID tag.

data to perform a manual sort as materials are checked in. For example, as an item is checked in, the shelving area that it should be returned to appears on-screen. This location information can be displayed in both SIP-based systems as well as direct RFID to ILS systems such as the one shown below.

Location information can also be stored in the database. If shelving location appears on the native ILS check-in screen, the direct RFID to ILS approach would be preferred. If it does not appear or is not stored in the ILS check-in software, a SIP-based system may be the only way to achieve this functionality.

If the objective is to simply check in as many items as quickly as possible without concern for sorting, other than pulling out "hold" materials, the processing of multiple items in a stack can greatly expedite the returns throughput. If returns are processed in batches, as opposed to checking in materials at the same time as they are delivered from patrons, some vendors provide a utility that allows a staff person to determine whether all items have been read without even looking at a computer screen. Unlike check out where the number of items that are placed on the reader will vary from patron to patron, during batch check in, the library may predetermine a number that will be placed on the reader at any one time. If, for instance, the number used is five, the system will alert the operator audibly if it detects fewer or more than five items, aborting the process until the correct number of tags is detected by the reader. Using this SIP-based solution, the operator can quickly pull those materials that have no tag or whose tags have been damaged. At the same time, should any item in a stack be on reserve, the system automatically sounds an alert and prints a holds ticket. So as long as five and only five items are

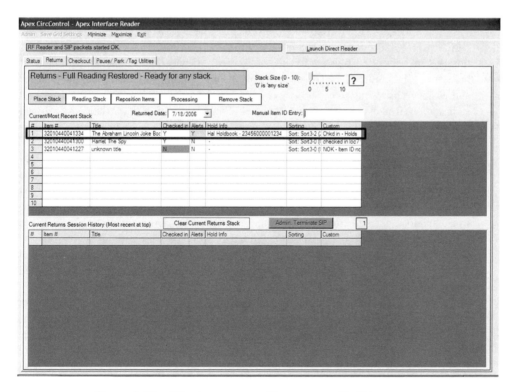

Figure 3.19. SIP returns screen with counter and hold item.

placed on the reader and as long as there are no holds, the operator may process stack after stack without ever looking at the screen. This "blind" methodology utilizes the SIP-based circulation software provided by the RFID vendor and not the native ILS system.

3.2.4   Patron Self Check-Out Stations

Patron self-service check-out kiosks have been used in libraries since the early 1990s. Libraries have been allowing patrons to check out their own materials long before grocery stores and retail establishments installed self-service item scanning and payment. RFID technology has been used for decades in warehousing, transportation, and other industries. However, libraries are leading the way in individual item tagging and changing, and, among other things, how business is conducted in self-service environments. Success in a self check-out context can be measured by the percentage of circulations that flow through it, with the goal of coming as close as possible to 100%. There are many factors that contribute to success including (but not limited to) location, staff commitment, fine and fee policies and the ability of the station to accept payments, how materials are secured (if at all), and ease of use. Lengthy expositions can be written about the benefits and pitfalls of each factor. Libraries are advised to consider their ramifications fully when implementing self service, regardless of whether RFID technology is used or not. We concentrate here, however, only on those areas that distinguish self check-out in an RFID environment from self check-out in a bar-code environment.

In the absence of RFID technology, self-service charging requires the scanning of each bar code on each item just as it is done at a staff circulation station. Patrons, like staff, must locate the bar-code label before it can be scanned. They often confuse the UPC or ISBN bar code with the library bar code. This presents less of a challenge if library item bar-code labels are located consistently—placed in the same location on all materials. If labels are placed on outside covers, both finding and scanning them is faster and easier. While consistent and convenient bar-code placement makes life easier at a staff station, it is even more critical at a self check-out station. Experience has shown that, all it can take is a single unpleasant experience to dissuade a patron from ever trying self service again.

Bar-code location is even more important in libraries using EM loss-prevention EAS systems, such as 3M's TattleTape® system. In addition to checking an item out in the database, its security strip must be deactivated or, to be more precise, desensitized. At staff stations, this is usually done in a separate step from bar-code scanning. To facilitate usage and to conceal the mechanism of the security system from potential thieves, to the greatest extent possible, it is best that tag desensitization be done without the patron having to perform a separate task to deactivate the security. If the bar code is situated so that the item's security strip is aligned properly with the station's desensitizer when placed under the scanner, no extra security deactivation step is needed. Because EM security strips are normally inserted into spines or deep between pages, book spines must be up against the desensitizer when an instruction is received from the ILS indicating that the item has been approved for check out. If, for some reason, this does not happen, the security strip will not be properly desensitized and will set off the alarm when passing through exit gates.

Many EM compatible self check-out systems incorporate desensitizers that allow some degree of variability in bar-code placement on print materials as well as on other nonmagnetic media, such as CDs and DVDs. Some systems require that magnetic media, such as videocassettes and audio cassettes, be handled separately; others allow all items to be handled in an identical fashion. Nevertheless, even in the best of EM worlds, consistent bar-code placement is a must.

Libraries with traditional RF security as well as libraries with no EAS system at all need not be concerned with the orientation of bar-code labels relative to book spines. Placement consistency throughout the collection does, however, make a great difference in the ability of staff and more importantly, the uninitiated patron, to find bar codes. If an RF security system is in use, patrons are instructed to insert the individual receipt printed for each checked-out item into its book pocket. A specially manufactured receipt paper detunes the signal of the RF security tag located beneath the pocket so that no alarms are sounded at the exit. This multistep process is considered complicated and/or burdensome by some library users. Others who simply ignore the instructions and do not insert receipts into pockets suffer the embarrassment of unwittingly setting off the security alarm. At the same time, the workings of the library security are made obvious to the public. Readily available detuning receipts may be moved from one item to another, providing thieves with an easy mechanism with which to ply their trade.

In comparison to bar-code-based systems, RFID-enabled self check-out stations facilitate usage in a number of ways:

- There is no need to locate bar codes and there is no possibility that a UPC or ISBN bar code will be confused with a library item bar code.
- Since an RFID tag can be read in any orientation, there is no requirement for exact placement of the item under a bar-code scanner.
- With rare exceptions, security deactivation occurs as items are charged. No separate steps are needed and there is little possibility that exit gates will sound an alarm when they should not.
- Instead of checking out books one at a time, patrons can check out stacks of books all at the same time.

There are clear advantages to self check-out in an RFID environment as compared to a bar-code environment, particularly when there is materials security involved. The power of RFID comes, however, with its own particular set of potential pitfalls to be addressed. RFID vendors should be asked the following questions:

- How does the system handle a mixed collection in which not all materials have RFID tags?
- Even when the library's entire collection is tagged, is there an accommodation for materials that come from other branches or other systems?
- Is the system configurable so that a library may choose between allowing multiple items to be checked out simultaneously and requiring that items be processed individually?
- Do the system's instructions make clear how RFID materials are handled differently from bar-coded items?
- What does the system do when one item of a stack may not be checked out?
- How does the system handle tag collisions, items without tags, items with unreadable tags, or any other situation where not all materials intended for check out are detected by the RFID reader?
- How does the system handle situations where an item not intended for check out is in close enough proximity to the scanning area that it is detected by the RFID reader?
- Is there such a thing as too fast?
- Does the system handle CDs and DVDs differently from other materials?

For a variety of reasons, some materials in the library will not have RFID tags. Some may have been missed during the initial conversion process while others may be on inter-library loan from another library. It is also not unusual for libraries to convert their collections to RFID over a period of years, during which time they will want to be able to use RFID to secure the expensive and/or most likely-to-be-stolen materials. Libraries should therefore look for a flexible self check-out system that "grows" as the migration to RFID progresses and one that takes into account non-RFID tagged materials even after the migration is complete.

For example, in the first phase, patrons might be instructed to check out all items against bar codes; the RFID tags in those materials serve an EAS function only, and their security bits are turned off with a successful charge. As more of the collection is tagged, the library may start using RFID for circulation purposes but may instruct patrons to put only one item on the reader at a time. If it cannot be read, the system instructs the patron to scan the bar code. Finally, after the entire collection has been converted, patrons are allowed to check out a stack of items all at one time. But, as we noted earlier, even then, accommodation should be made for those materials that do not have an RFID tag.

Patrons do not know which items have RFID tags and which do not, or which tags have been damaged or simply cannot be read for one reason or another. At a manned staff station, a trained library employee quickly recognizes the various potential problems and can easily take the proper steps to resolve them. At self check-out, however, the system must recognize the problem and instruct the patron to take the necessary steps to correct it.

The most popular approach taken is to list on screen all items that the RFID reader has detected and to require that the patron confirm that the information displayed is correct. The items are checked out only after the patron has made this confirmation and, in the case of R/W systems, only then are the security bits of the materials in the reader area disarmed. If the patron does not confirm the items, some systems ask the patron to place items on the reader one at a time while other systems simply instruct the patron to call for help. But in either case, the patron is relied upon to act to complete the process. Unfortunately, in today's world of fine print and Internet transactions that require mouse click after mouse click to complete a transaction, we have all become conditioned to quickly hit the "continue" button with little regard to what is shown on the screen. Therefore, relying on patrons to properly confirm all the items they are checking out and verify that only those items they want to check out appear on the screen is risky business. If the patron does perform as instructed and calls for staff help when what appears on screen does not match with what has been placed on the reader, he or she will expect help to come immediately. If it does not, the likelihood the patron will use self check-out the next time visiting the library is seriously diminished.

A number of possible scenarios may result from a patron confirming the number of items when it is not correct. The most likely occurrence is that materials without RFID tags leave the library without record. If an item with an RFID tag is not detected, it is likely to set off the alarm at the exit gate. In a WORM environment where security is database driven, the alarm will go off because all the items will not appear in the list of checked-out materials. In an R/W environment, if an RFID tag is not read, it is unlikely that its EAS security bit will be turned off. In both cases, the patron will suffer from unnecessary embarrassment since there was a good faith attempt to check everything out properly. Such an experience certainly creates a disincentive to future self check-out usage.

On the other hand, although less likely than the scenario described above, it is possible for the RFID reader to pick up an RFID tag of an item that the patron does not desire to check out. This happens when an item is placed accidentally in too close a proximity to the reader. In this instance, the item is charged to the patron's account despite the fact that it never left the library.

Libraries should note possible actions to be taken in those cases where the patron sees that there is a mismatch and requests assistance. One possibility is to instruct the user to remove all materials from the reading zone and check out items one at a time. If the system does not detect an RFID tag, it can instruct the patron to scan the item's bar code. More commonly, the system simply directs the user to request assistance. To ensure that assistance is provided promptly, a staff person may be assigned to monitor a few self check-out stations. In some libraries, there is a dedicated staff person at each station. The latter scenario is most likely to be found in combination stations featuring dual monitors, one facing the patron and the other facing a staff person. These stations allow staff to take over and complete the transaction. Whether it is a one-to-one, one-to-two, one-to-three, or one-to-four staff to patron ration, what results is best described as a staff-assisted self-service system. As a result, some libraries have discovered that the anticipated reduction in staff time dedicated to charging transactions as a result of RFID implementation has proven to be illusory.

There is an alternative to the "patron match" approach that eliminates, except for rare exceptions, mistakes of the type noted above. In this "system match" or "pre-count" method, the user specifies the number of items placed in the reading area. The system, in turn, responds to the user accordingly. If the reader detects the same number of items specified, the transaction moves forward; those materials are checked out to the patron, unless, of course, there is an item in the stack that may not, for some reason, be circulated. In that case, the user is instructed to remove the "offending" item from the read area so that the security bits on the remaining items can be deactivated.

If the system detects more tags than the number of items the patron has specified, it notifies the patron and requests a recount. If the system detects fewer tags than the number of items specified, the patron is instructed to rotate and spread the items across the reading area. If the system still fails to detect all items, it reverts automatically to "one at a time mode" and the patron is requested to check out each item separately. The one-at-a-time process may be set up so that if the RFID reader fails to detect an RFID tag, it then instructs the user to scan the item's bar-code label.

Note that the active counting required of the patron in the system match approach eliminates many of the potential pitfalls of the patron match methodology that requires only a confirmation of the items displayed on screen. While the system match approach demands a bit more of the patron, the elimination of the potential problems makes for a better overall user experience.

Keep in mind that the operational objectives of a self check-out station are not necessarily identical to those of a staff station. At a staff station, speed is paramount and every attempt should be made to streamline the process, keeping in mind that a trained employee is watching out for the quirks of the system. At a self check-out station, speed plays second fiddle to accuracy. A staff person may handle hundreds of transactions a day; however, it is rare for a patron to come into the library more than once a week. Library patrons, like customers everywhere, do not like to wait in line. But once the process begins and it is reasonably quick, easy, and trouble free, patrons will not be impatient. After all, patrons are not timing the transaction with a stopwatch. The time savings gained by not having to locate and scan bar codes individually more than makes up for the time required to ensure that everything has been done properly.

There is actually a point at which fast is too fast. That point is reached whenever the transaction proceeds so quickly that the patron does not have time to respond or by virtue of experience with the system, the patron ignores messages from the system. As discussed earlier in the section on tags, check-out transactions are generally fastest in WORM environments where there is no need to turn off EAS bits since security is database dependent. Users at staff or self check-out stations need only wave items across the RFID reader to check them out, as opposed to R/W systems, where the user must leave items in place until EAS bits are deactivated. This works well as long as patrons wait for the message returned from the system indicating that all the materials have been checked out properly. However, experienced users quickly stop paying attention to what is on screen as they pass materials over the reader. A message that comes back stating, for instance, that an item is a noncirculating reference material that may not be checked out is easily ignored. When the patron exits through the security gates, that item will set off the alarm. The additional time required to check out items in an EAS R/W environment is time well spent if the system forces patrons to pay attention to the on-screen messages and avoid problems exiting the library.

Regardless of the RFID system used, it is helpful if the patron's receipt specifies not only what has been checked out but also what has failed to check out. When the security gate alarm does go off, staff can politely ask to see the receipt. Security systems that provide real-time item identification can also be used to accomplish this objective, but as we point out in the section about RFID loss prevention, the reliability of this functionality drops when there are multiple tags in the field.

We now return to the Achilles heel of RFID, CDs, and DVDs. In the section on tags, we discussed at length the challenges presented by the metallic content of disks and the proximity of one to another when stacked, or, even worse, in multipart sets. In that discussion, we pointed out that the donut-style tags that can be applied directly to disks do not read reliably at RFID security gates. Wherever possible, when using these tags, placing more than one CD or DVD on a reader should be avoided during circulation processes. Libraries with serious theft concerns may have no choice but to use locking security "keepers," placing standard rectangular RFID tags on CD jewel boxes and DVD cases. This not only secures the collection more effectively but also allows multiple items to be stacked on a reader. Unfortunately, these security cases must be unlocked and, in some systems, removed before the patron can be sent on his way. This extra step is a time-consuming nuisance for staff. Moreover, it can eliminate a large percentage of potential self check-out usage, particularly when considering how important AV materials have become in most public libraries.

Some libraries, including the Warren-Newport Public Library, place their self check-out stations on the circulation desk and allow patrons access to the AV unlocking keys so that they can open security cases themselves. Since the circulation desk is manned at all times, the hope is that patrons will unlock these cases only after they have checked out the materials. Clearly, such an approach is subject to abuse, and as this book is being written, Warren-Newport is looking to its RFID vendor to provide an interface with the self check-out system that will prevent security cases from being unlocked unless the enclosed items have been checked out.

Some vendors have developed just such an interface to work either with locking cases specifically designed for this purpose or with cases, such as the Kwik Case™, that a library may already be using. A special unlocking device is integrated into each self check-out station, or a separate security case release station may be used. Libraries should take a number of factors into consideration when examining the available options, including, of course, cost, ease of use by the patron, and the impenetrability of the locking cases themselves. Like most things in life, you usually get what you pay for; the less expensive the cases, the more likely they are to be opened even without a special key.

As important as AV materials, may be, both in terms of their security and circulation activity, how they are handled by the RFID system and at self check-out in particular is but one factor among many that a library needs to consider when selecting its vendor. As we noted in our discussion in the tags section, the "Ipodization" of the world may make the circulation of CDs and DVDs a moot point within a relatively short time.

3.2.5 Automated Returns and Sorting

This section discusses the use of RFID readers for automating the return of materials. There are two separate components to this automation: automated returns using either a book drop or returns kiosk, and automated sorting systems. Depending on the volume of returns and the size of the library, none, one, or both components should be considered. We will discuss the features of each and their associated benefits.

Automated returns.

RFID is a powerful tool for automating returns in a way that was never possible previously. Libraries can choose to have RFID readers built into their book return chutes. Book return manufacturers also provide freestanding drops designed specifically for RFID. In addition to including brackets to hold readers and antennae, these book drops are also available with the necessary heaters and air conditioners to ensure that extreme temperatures do not damage equipment. Some libraries may want the additional security and patron interface functionality that come with a check-in kiosk. In all cases, electrical power and a network connection with SIP are required.

Standard RFID Book Drop. The basic setup of an RFID book drop is simple. Generally, an RFID antenna is mounted in a bracket directly under the book return chute so that RFID tags are read as materials slide through. Communicating through SIP, these items are discharged in real time and the patron's record is immediately updated. Beyond these basics, there are differences in what various RFID systems can do and what features they offer.

While all systems can read tags without difficulty as they pass quickly through the chute, systems vary greatly in their ability to write to tags in motion. This is of no consequence in a WORM environment since security functionality is database dependent; as an item is returned, it is removed from the list of checked-out items in the RFID server. In EAS R/W environments, the security bit must be reactivated by writing to the tag. Most R/W systems are incapable of consistently turning on security bits at the average speed that materials pass through a book return chute. Because of this inability, it becomes necessary to reactivate security bits in a separate process. If reactivation is done manually, some vendors offer a utility that provides shelving location at the same time. Alternatively, instead of delivering materials directly into a bin, the library may choose to direct them onto a slow conveyor equipped with a separate RFID reader that turns on security bits on the way to a bin. If a conveyor is being considered for the single purpose of turning on security bits, the library may want to consider taking the next step and installing a sorting system. We will address sorting systems in the next section.

At least one manufacturer has developed a tag whose security bit can be turned on simultaneously with the reading of the tag. Systems that use these tags state with confidence that all RFID-tagged items that have found their way to book return bins have active security bits.

Most systems offer libraries the option of printing holds tickets as items are checked in, and some will alert staff with an audible signal anytime something on reserve is checked in. This audible signal is valuable if there is a staff person in the immediate vicinity who can pull the reserved item from the bin before it is buried beneath other materials. If an immediate pull is not possible, for example, when the library is closed, holds tickets should be matched with checked-in materials after they have been placed in call number order on a book truck. Some libraries may find it faster and easier, however, to discharge items a second time and print holds tickets at that point. With this procedure, the issue of turning on security bits in the book drop becomes a moot point since EAS reactivation can be done at the same time. If the system is set up to provide shelving location information, this data can also be displayed.

Libraries may ask, "If we go to the trouble of installing automated check in, why not offer patrons a receipt as well?" In Europe, as well as other places in the world, it is common practice to provide returns receipts for everything, not only in libraries but also in video rental stores. The customer-friendly environment found in North America has, at least up until now, instilled in patrons sufficient confidence to believe that they will be trusted in the event of a dispute. As a result, very few request or demand returns receipts, unless their credit card is to be credited. While the most cost-efficient approach

Figure 3.20.   Library Mate™ internal book return.

is to require patrons who want receipts to return materials to a staff person during business hours, or to allow a receipt to be printed from the Internet, some libraries want to offer this as a 24/7 service through the automated returns system. There are costs to pay, both direct and indirect.

Receipt-printing functionality requires, in addition to the printer and the paper, some type of user interface so that the patron can indicate when the last item was inserted and choose whether a receipt was wanted or not. Whether this is done with a key pad or touch screen, the library incurs the cost of the equipment, the custom installation, and whatever additional software charge the vendor may add. Additionally, there is the ongoing expense of the receipt paper itself. A less obvious cost may result from user discontent when the system goes down, the receipt printer is not working or runs out of paper, or when the patron drops a non-RFID tagged item into the drop. If a patron puts five items into the chute, he or she expects to receive a receipt showing all five items.

Book Return Kiosk. If, in addition to providing receipts, the library desires to show patron status information and/or add to its building security, a kiosk-like return is a better choice than the traditional book drop described above. Such a kiosk can provide all the information that is made available at the self check-out, such as on-reserve materials currently available and fines owed. It is also possible to outfit the kiosk with payment acceptance capability. As an extra security precaution, the kiosk may be set up to require the insertion of a patron card before a door opens allowing access to returns platform.

Figure 3.21. Library Mate™ external book return.

Instead of a returns slot, kiosks usually have a flat conveyor. Should someone insert something that the system does not recognize, the conveyor reverses course and returns it to the user; the receipt shows only those materials that were accepted. Most systems also provide libraries with the option of reading bar-code labels in addition to RFID tags.

Kiosks are not as fast as traditional book drops. In addition to requiring additional steps, materials must be inserted one at a time, and the patron must wait for the system to process one item before proceeding to the next. Patrons who are accustomed to simply "dropping and running" may find the extra demands of the kiosk to be an unwelcome nuisance. In contrast, an RFID-enabled book drop requires no change in customer behavior at all.

Automated materials handling (sorting).

Automated materials handling (AMH) systems have been improving productivity in warehouse, shipping, and other industries for many years. Over the course of the past decade, they have also begun to make an impact on the library world. While RFID is not required for sorting, it has the potential to significantly improve the process and reduce costs. Unlike bar codes that require exact positioning to be read, the key advantage of RFID tags is that they can be read in any location, in any orientation, and at virtually any speed. Depending on the RFID system used, no extra step or equipment is needed to reactivate the security component. As we noted above, an RFID-enabled return can be instituted that requires no change in patron behavior. Libraries may therefore find that the fastest return on investment (ROI) they receive from RFID implementation comes from AMH.

An entire book could be devoted to the subject of AMH in a library environment and to the different options and features available, not to mention the physical design and operation of the equipment itself. We will focus here on some of the critical aspects that libraries should consider when AMH is implemented in the context of an RFID project.

First, without RFID, a kiosk-like return is the only available option that ensures that materials are placed correctly on the induction conveyor so that the bar-code label is properly aligned with the scanner. With RFID, the library may even continue to use its existing book drop, with no retrofitting required, placing the RFID reader in a conveyor

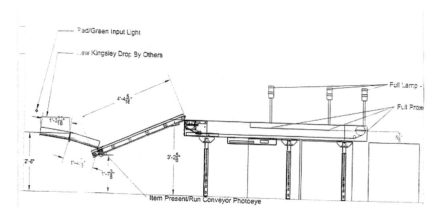

Figure 3.22. Automated sorting system.

that moves materials from the book drop chute to the sorter. Warren-Newport's RFID-enabled sorting system was installed in such a way.

The faceplate of a book drop should have a simple slot for one-handed insertion as opposed to a pull-out drawer that requires two hands, one to pull out the drawer and the other to insert materials. Accurate sorting obviously works best when items are inserted one at a time. People do that naturally when inserting items into a slot; on the other hand, they try to stuff as much as they can into a pull-out drawer. Most sorters are fast enough to keep up with users inserting materials at a natural pace. However, a sensor connected to a light that flashes when the system is prepared to accept the next item is an inexpensive and effective way to keep the system and user in sync.

Unlike a kiosk where unrecognized materials are returned to the user, all materials inserted into a book drop remain in the library. Therefore, one of the bins of the sorting system must be designated as an exception bin. Any item without a tag, with a damaged tag, whose location cannot be determined, or which is rejected by the system for any other reason is directed to this bin for further examination and processing. If each item in a multipart set is tagged individually, a properly designed system will send the item to the exception bin if it fails to read all parts of the set. A well-designed system should also take into account that inevitably there will be items that are on top of each other or too close to one another for the system to sort into separate locations. A poorly designed system will grab the information from the first tag it reads and send any items that happen to be in the vicinity into the same bin location. A well-designed system recognizes that more than one tag is in the reading zone and directs all items to the exception bin.

Because RFID allows items to be read regardless of orientation, book drop-style sorting systems are not ideal for delivering materials onto book trucks so that all items are positioned neatly facing the same direction with their spines out. To solve this problem, equipment that senses the orientation of a book and turns it as needed is available. However, the cost and reliability of such equipment should be examined closely. Book drop sorting systems accomplish their core mission simply and effectively without additional bells and whistles. They are also relatively inexpensive, and because they simply direct materials into standard bins, they are both easy to operate and trouble free. Libraries that want more sophisticated systems that automatically align materials on the shelf of a book truck will want to consider kiosk-style returns. And, as was explained earlier, kiosks offer bar-code-reading capability, patron interface features, and enhanced security.

Some libraries want to direct materials to a sorter from more than one induction point. This capability is available with book drop and kiosk returns, the latter being more complex and expensive. Each induction point requires a complete kiosk, a significant expense. In addition, because each item is read and checked in at the kiosk, it must be tracked all along whatever paths the conveyor may take to ensure that, when it arrives at the sorter, it is delivered to the proper location. Accurate tracking of materials flowing from different directions into a central distribution point requires sophisticated programming and equipment. On the other hand, materials conveyed from standard book drops are not read until they are within just a few feet of the sorter. The RFID and accompanying computer hardware required is no greater for an automated materials handling system with multiple induction points than it is for a system with only one book drop. The only additional components needed, beyond the book drops and the conveyors, are sensors placed at convergence points on the conveyor to prevent materials from bunching up.

Sorting systems can be configured with hundreds of bins. Space and budget considerations prevent all but a few libraries from installing systems with even as many as 10 bins.

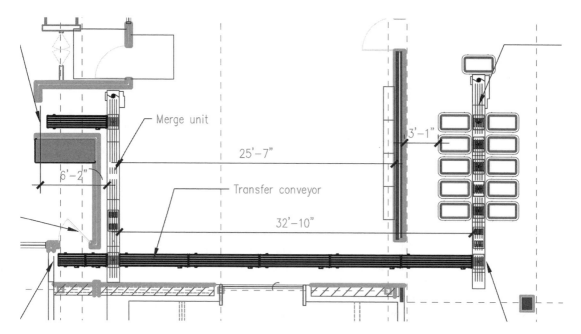

Figure 3.23.   Sorting system.

It is important to remember, however, that the greatest value comes with the first three bins—one for holds, one for materials to be re-shelved within the library, and one for everything else (the exception bin). The identification and separation of holds is an exceptional workflow improvement. Patrons benefit from the fact that their reserve items are available within seconds from the time the reserved materials are returned to the library. Other additional sorts above and beyond these first three are gravy.

3.2.6   Electronic Article Surveillance and Security Gates

In the section about tags, we discussed the different ways that materials loss prevention can be incorporated into an RFID environment:

- No RFID-based security system
- Server-based system utilizing item identification
- RTF utilizing EAS security bit
- TTF utilizing EAS security bit

A thorough understanding of the differences between approaches is paramount to properly evaluating competing systems; we encourage the reader to review the tags section on EAS security again. Here, we address issues not covered in the tags section, ones that, for the most part, pertain to all RFID security systems.

Installation.

All security gates, regardless of the technology used, require electrical power. If affixed directly into flooring, electrical conduit needs to run beneath or on the floor to each of the gates. Some vendors offer pedestals with secured base plates under them, allowing cables to be run under the pedestal. WORM systems that are database dependent for security and R/W EAS systems that offer an item identification option also require a network connection to each gate. While all RFID vendors will fine-tune gate installation as necessary, some recommend that physical installation and electrical wiring be done by qualified local contractors of the library's choosing according to specifications provided by the vendor. It is recommended that gates be kept out of direct sunlight that can cause wood finishes to fade and plastic encasings to crack.

Interference.

All radio signals are subject to interference. At the most basic level, the FCC strictly regulates publicly used frequencies to prevent encroachment and the restricted range of RFID readers limits interference of other types. However, the greater the reading range, the greater the likelihood of there being interference. Attention should therefore be paid in particular to RFID security gates, where reading ranges may be three or four times that of readers used in other library applications.

The most likely source of interference is proximity to metal. Different amounts and types of metal may affect security gates differently, and most vendors will say that it is impossible to state with certainty how high the likelihood of interference is until the gates are installed. It is therefore critical that security pedestal placement follows vendor installation guidelines strictly. To be safe, do not install gates closer than 2 feet from metal door frames.

The second likely source of interference is other electronic devices. Because the power of those devices may vary, it is best to maintain a radius of 8 feet around the gates and away from other electronic equipment (an electronic-free zone).

False alarms.

Interference usually results in a failure to read all tags that are within the interrogation zone. However, interference may also result in false alarms. Generally speaking, proper system tuning prevents false alarms. However, there is a trade-off between sensitivity and false alarms. It is possible to lower a system's sensitivity to the point where there are no false alarms whatsoever. In all likelihood, doing so will substantially lower the system's overall tag-detection capabilities. In an effort to maintain as high a sensitivity level as possible without generating false alarms, some manufacturers equip security pedestals with sensors that prevent gates from emitting signals unless movement in the interrogation zone or weight exerted on a foot plate is detected. Overall, the false alarm rate of RFID systems is lower than EM systems and traditional RF systems that have been used in libraries.

Read range.

Most RFID security-gate readers have a range of 18 inches. Two pedestals create a 3-foot aisle. The read range of WORM systems is usually greater, sometimes as much as 24 inches creating aisle widths of 4 feet. It is important to remember, however, that a greater read range does not necessarily translate into a more reliable detection level. As was discussed in the tags section, the "pick rate" of an RFID security system is a function, in good measure, of the EAS methodology used. And as we pointed out earlier, R/W systems do a better job detecting EAS security bits than they do reading bar-code numbers since reading a 14-digit number is always more challenging than reading a single bit.

Dead zones.

The pick rate, the average number of tags that the system detects under random position and orientation testing, is also affected by dead zones. While gates may perform well when a tag at belt height is passed between them, there may be performance degradation when the tag is at the head or foot level.

Item identification.

As has been stated before, WORM system tags do not have EAS security bits that are turned on and off. Security relies instead on capturing the specific item IDs of those materials that have not been properly checked out. A standard or optional feature offered by most vendors with R/W EAS bit solutions, whether RTF or TTF based, is the ability to generate item ID information for those items that set off the security gates. After addressing the question of how well any system consistently extracts complete item identification numbers from RFID tags, the question of what the library does with that information can be answered.

The library may use the data collected in batch form for inventory purposes, producing a report of those materials that have left the premises without being checked out. In a WORM environment, the accuracy of the report is only diminished by the extent to which the gates fail to successfully read all items passing through the interrogation zones. In an R/W EAS security-bit environment, the accuracy of the report may be further affected if security bits were not properly deactivated even though the materials were properly checked out. As we have noted previously, this can happen because the process of writing information to a tag is more difficult than that of reading information

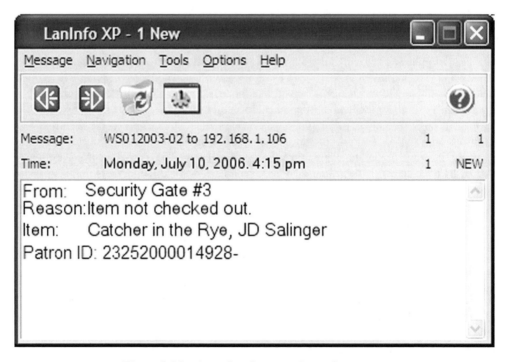

Figure 3.24. Item identification software for security gates.

from a tag. From an inventory perspective, the fact that the report may contain items that were properly charged has no bearing if that report is run against the list of checked-out materials. However, by compiling data on those items whose security bits fail to deactivate during check out, information regarding this aspect of RFID system performance can be discerned.

Libraries can also choose to display item identification in real time. By connecting to the database via SIP, the bar-code number is used to produce title information. Staff and, if the library chooses, patrons may see the title of the item that set off the alarm in real time. There is no need to examine each item that the patron may have at the backpack to determine which one set off the gates; that information is already known.

AV materials.

We refer you again to the section on tags in this chapter for a full discussion of what some call the Achilles heel of RFID, security of CDs and DVDs.

Optional features.

There are a number of features that some vendors include as standard with their security systems while others offer as options. These include custom finishes, built-in patron counters and connections to CCTV, voice prompts ("Please return to the circulation desk"), and other external electronic devices that might be triggered by a security alert. Other than item identification described above, these features are generally available with any security system and are not specific to RFID.

Servicing of gates.

Most components of an RFID system are easily replaced should they malfunction. As such, it may never be necessary for a vendor's technician to actually set foot in the library in order to fix a problem. This is not the case with security gates. Libraries must therefore be certain that their support contracts include on-site servicing of gates.

3.2.7   Stack Maintenance

Shelf-reading devices collect inventory data, search for specific items, and identify mis-shelved materials. Depending on the system, these tasks can be performed either individually or simultaneously. In addition, at least one manufacturer provides a shelf reader that turns on EAS security bits while simultaneously performing the other functions.

Shelf-reading applications.

Shelf-reading capabilities open up the option to more accurately track inventory, to assure that items are properly shelved, to locate missing items, and, generally, to eliminate the manual process of having to remove books from the stacks in order to accomplish all these tasks. The following sections discuss the various shelf-reading applications that are available with RFID.

Inventory.

The most basic function of a shelf-reading system is the collection of inventory data. As the reader is passed or waved along the shelf, it extracts bar-code numbers from RFID tags. This data may be stored and uploaded in batch mode to the library's database or it may be transmitted in real time, usually via a wireless connection.

There are two important differences between taking inventory by scanning bar codes and by reading RFID tags: how the data is collected and the speed with which it is collected. From the operator's perspective, both the process and the speed are of importance. Data collection with RFID requires significantly less time and the time spent collecting the data is less physically taxing since materials are not handled manually. From the ILS perspective, it is important that the data is not transmitted at a speed faster than the database has the capacity to absorb. Some RFID shelf readers are so fast that a buffer may be required to ensure that the database is not overwhelmed. It is generally recommended that data be collected and uploaded in batch mode at a later time, just as is currently done with most bar-code-based inventory readers.

Whether information is transmitted to the ILS in batch mode or in real time, the RFID vendor must ensure that the data is presented to the database in a format that it is designed to accept. While some RFID vendors offer their own inventory reporting software, where available, libraries will find it preferable to use the inventory module that is part of their ILS.

Search.

The stack maintenance system supplied by the RFID vendor should include an item search module. The library may input item identification information directly into the shelf-reading software. Usually, the library generates a list or report from its ILS that includes bar-code numbers and titles. Once generated, this list is uploaded to the shelf reader. Just as it was necessary in the case of inventory for the RFID vendor to ensure that the information transmitted to the ILS is in a compatible format, the vendor must provide the library with the necessary tools to translate the data that is uploaded from the ILS into a format that is compatible with the RFID software.

The following describes a typical search scenario. Details, of course, may vary from system to system. When the shelf reader identifies a bar-code number from the search list, it alerts the operator with an audible and/or visual signal. The bar-code number that was found and its title appear on screen. Further tag reading is interrupted until the user indicates that whatever actions are called for regarding the search item have been taken. Remember that RFID readers do not emit linear fields that can be directed to narrowly confined areas. (Any vendor's claim that a reader is capable of directly identifying a single item amongst an entire shelf of items should be viewed with suspicion.) Rather, a reader picks up any tag that is in any part of the interrogation zone. The size of that zone varies with different vendors' readers and it also may be affected by how the reader is held. Typically, that zone encompasses 6 inches on both sides of the reader. Remember, as well, the random nature of RFID means that a reader may detect a book 6 inches away before it detects one that is 3 inches away or even 1 inch away. Therefore, when the reader detects an item in the search list, that item may be as far as 6 inches away from the reader's position when the alert is sounded. That is where the title information comes into play. The operator searches the interrogation zone by title to find the identified item.

As stated, the above is a typical scenario; the details may vary from vendor to vendor. Some systems do not alert the user each time a search item is discovered. Instead, when the search process is concluded, a report is generated that shows where on the shelves items in the search group are located. Then, a worker can return to the stacks with a cart or basket to pull the items. This two-step approach addresses those who would prefer to focus on shelf reading without interruption and would rather not carry a basket or push a cart at the same time. Overall shelf maintenance should be faster, however, with the one-step process, particularly if a fast and accurate reader is used. As we will discuss later in this section, the greatest speed and accuracy may be delivered from a wand connected to a separate RFID coupler powered from a wall outlet or from a heavy-duty external battery. Also, some systems work with laptop computers as opposed to hand-held PDA-type devices that have small built-in batteries. If the system requires a cart to hold a coupler, a laptop, a battery, or even all three, that same cart may be used to hold the materials pulled from shelves.

Looking for missing items is the most common use of search functionality, and missing item report generation is generally a standard feature of a library's ILS. A library may choose to weed its collection by doing a search for materials that have not circulated over the course of a specified period. As long as data can be entered into the stack maintenance software, whether it is generated from the ILS or input manually, that data can be used to create a search list. Some systems may even allow multiple lists to be searched simultaneously.

What should be searched for, when searches should be done, and whether they should be done simultaneously with other shelf-reading operations or even simultaneously with other searches need to be addressed by each library based on its individual needs. Remember that while RFID is a powerful tool, like all technologies, it may not always be the best solution for a particular library. For example, some have suggested that an RFID shelf reader be used on a daily basis to pull holds. While this may provide some satisfaction that this expensive equipment is being put to work each and every day, it will be discovered quickly that holds can be more rapidly pulled the old-fashioned way. RFID is terrific for finding things where the location of the item is unknown. When the location is known, a manual search against a printed shelf list order is much faster and easier. This would be true even if RFID readers could stop an operator at the exact spot that a specific item is located (which, as stated, they cannot).

Identification of mis-shelved materials.

The missing-item search process is designed to find those materials that were not found when needed. Conversely, the process of identifying mis-shelved materials is designed to find any item that is not where it should be, or at least outside the general area where it should be. When using this functionality, the basics of RFID technology need to be clearly understood in order to properly weigh the plusses and minuses of different systems and how they address this task.

In our discussion of search, we emphasized that an RFID shelf reader can be used effectively to alert an operator to the presence of a single book, even in the midst of a row or stack of many others. However, we also pointed out that the reader is not equipped to physically direct the operator to that individual item since it reads everything within the interrogation zone and not necessarily in order. The operator locates the identified item by title searching in the area around the reader when the alert is sounded (or in the case of the two-step search process, when items are identified from a printed list). The physics of RFID apply equally to any attempt made to determine whether an item is not shelved in its proper location. That said, vendors have taken different approaches while addressing this technical constraint.

Essentially, there is a trade-off between a narrow interrogation zone on one hand and speed and power on the other. In other words, a smaller interrogation zone may be achieved but only at the cost of speed and, in some cases, tag-reading accuracy.

Some vendors claim their shelf readers can determine whether an item is shelved as little as 5 places, or approximately five inches, away from its proper location. To do this, however, the reader must be moved slowly across shelves. This constrained speed helps to control the interrogation field and allows the operator to react to an alert while the reader is still in front of the mis-shelved item. Vendors also limit the width of the reading zone by reducing the power of the reader. Ideally, that power could be reduced to a point where the reader is capable of only picking up the tag that is directly in front of it. Practically, that would mean bringing the reader into virtual contact with the tag and that, of course, would mean pulling materials away from shelves, just as one does when taking inventory using bar-code labels. The reader must have power sufficient to detect tags that are found on materials, without, of course, having to touch or move them. That required power that inevitably extends the interrogation zone beyond any one item.

In an ideal world, where all materials are tagged exactly according to the vendor's instructions, not too high and not too far away from book spines, and where everything is flushed front and even on shelves, a reader would not need power above and beyond what is needed to read tags in their normative locations. The real world must account for sloppy tag application and sloppy shelves. An RFID shelf reader does this through increased power. This increased power results in better tag detection and allows the operator to work faster. The cost is a wider interrogation zone, perhaps as wide as half a shelf.

Librarians must ask themselves, "How mis-shelved should an item be before it is officially considered mis-shelved?" For those unwilling to accept anything but exact shelving, RFID, at least in the current state of its technology, may not be appropriate at all. Others, appreciating what RFID can do despite its imperfections, need to determine the acceptable degree of imperfection, recognizing that with more imperfection comes greater speed and greater tag-reading accuracy. Some would argue that as long as a book is on the right shelf, it is findable. Others would say that half a shelf, or approximately 36 inches, should be considered normative. One way or the other, all agree that when scanning shelves, patrons look both to the left and to the right of the proper call number locations if they do not find what they are looking for in the places where those items should be found. Furthermore, librarians can generally attest to the fact that even if everything were, by some miracle, in its exact right place at any moment in time, that perfection would last for only minutes, if not seconds.

This real-world analysis can be taken one step further by asking, "Even if the shelf reader could alert the operator or create a line item on a report every time it found something that was not in its exact proper location, would you want it to do so?" Many would respond as follows: "I want to know whenever an item is outside of the range where most people would find it." Librarians taking this flexible approach are rewarded with RFID shelf readers that detect close to 100% of all tagged items (nothing is perfect) and do so while moving at as fast a pace as the operator can comfortably move an arm.

Activation of EAS security bits.
In our discussion of automated discharge, we noted that RFID tags can be read while in motion without difficulty. In most cases, however, writing information to tags, including the turning on and off of EAS security bits, can only be done when both tag and reader are stationary or when tags or readers are moving at relatively slow speeds (slower than the average speed of a book traveling through a book return chute). At least one vendor has successfully overcome this limitation with a system that reactivates security bits as

quickly as it reads the information on tags. This technology has been incorporated into the vendor's shelf reader to turn on EAS bits at the same time that inventory, search, or identification of mis-shelved items is being done. Libraries using such a system know not only what is on their shelves but also that everything on their shelves is secured.

Shelf-reading performance.

Our discussion of shelf-reading applications, in particular search and mis-shelved item identification, addresses not only what the systems are designed to do but also some of the technological limitations that they confront. Here, we expound further on the issues previously raised and address other matters pertaining to reader performance.

Accuracy and speed.

In an RFID context, shelf-reading accuracy is a measure of a system's ability to detect and read all tags that are within the interrogation zone. Our discussions in the sections of the book dealing with tags and readers and, in particular, our discussions of tag collision and the special challenge of AV materials apply to shelf readers as well. As we saw in the previous sections dealing with other RFID applications, both the power and limitations of the technology need to be understood in order to create solutions that work in the real world. We described various techniques that different systems use to ensure that all materials in the RFID-reading zone, be it at a staff or patron self check-out station, are actually read. We noted the varying performance levels of the different approaches to loss prevention, but pointed out that no security system is foolproof and that a 95% "pick rate" should be considered excellent. If, however, a library's inventory procedure could only find 95% of the materials that were actually on the shelves, most would consider the entire exercise to be worthless. A shelf reader may be fast, have terrific features, be ergonomically designed, and even easy to use, but if it is not accurate, everything else is meaningless.

A measure of shelf-reading accuracy is meaningful only within the contexts of specific speeds and material types. The statement "The RFID shelf reader accurately reads 99.8% of materials on the shelf" tells us little. On the other hand, the statement "The RFID shelf reader accurately reads 99.8% of books one eight of an inch thick or thicker at a rate of 15 per second" is a true measure of its performance. A vendor's statements regarding the performance levels of various applications may well be true under very specific and usually ideal conditions. In the case of shelf reading, the ideal condition would probably include all books being at least 1 inch thick. And even then, accurate reading may allow no more than two or three reads a second.

RFID shelf readers do indeed exist that are capable of accurately reading close to 100% of books, whose thickness is one-eighth of an inch or more at a rate of 15 per second. As we explained in our discussion of search and identification of mis-shelved materials, this high-level performance uses a powerful reader that most likely requires electricity or an external heavy-duty battery. We also noted there that along with this power comes an expansion of the zone that needs to be visually scanned should there be an RFID-generated alert. The goal is to achieve as close to 100% read accuracy as possible without enlarging the interrogation zone to the point where it becomes unworkable. For example, it makes no sense to have a shelf reader so powerful that materials on the shelf below or behind are read. A read range of 12 inches, for example, could do just that. Fortunately, there are readers with ranges not exceeding 6 inches that are powerful enough to deliver real-world and world-class performance.

Memory, processing speed, and battery life.

As computer users are well aware, few things have advanced and continue to advance as rapidly as have the amount of computer memory and CPU speed. At the same time, components are getting smaller and smaller. As a result, it is virtually impossible to make definitive statements concerning shelf-reading capabilities in this regard. At the time of this writing, some vendors have determined that PDA-type devices are incapable of handling sufficient quantities of data and/or processing data quickly enough for their applications. In addition, these and other vendors have expressed concern about battery life since the reader may be used for long periods of time without interruption. Instead of offering a single-piece hand-held shelf reader that functions not only as an RFID antenna and coupler but also as a computer with screen, these vendors offer a shelf wand that connects via cable to a laptop computer. The RFID reader, as well as the computer, if desired, is powered from a wall outlet through an extension cord or from a heavy-duty rechargeable battery that rides on the cart along with the other equipment.

If shelf reading is an important benefit that the library anticipates achieving through RFID, it is imperative that decision makers see for themselves how each vendor's offering works in real-world conditions, making sure that it performs satisfactorily, particularly in the application the library deems to be most important. When total portability is clearly advantageous and when an application may require only limited memory and number crunching, an all-in-one hand-held device may be preferred. An all-in-one unit may also be the best when collecting usage information by scanning reference books left on tables before they are re-shelved. Otherwise, other factors should dictate what type of shelf reader is best, such as those noted previously, or the footprint and ergonomic factors that we address next.

Figure 3.25.   Shelf-reading system with cart.

Physical design.

A library considering RFID should analyze physical design from a number of perspectives. As we noted in our discussion of battery life, shelf readers are often used for long periods of time without interruption. Miniaturization of electronics now allows substantial power to be built into hand-held devices. If a hand-held reader passes the test for reading power, processing speed, memory, and battery life, the next step is to evaluate the equipment from an ergonomic perspective. Proper ergonomic design should allow an operator to work continuously with limited break time without fatigue or physical stress. Hand-held equipment must be lightweight, have a comfortable grip, and allow the user to scan all shelves, both high and low, with minimal reaching and bending. Screens should have fonts that are large enough to read without squinting, and operators should be able to input information, where necessary, without having to pass an Olympic test for fine motor skills coordination. Unfortunately, a true test of any of these measures requires use of the equipment for an extended period of time. What may appear to be a nonstressful procedure when repeated for only 10-minute time periods can be a nightmare of a job when done for hours on end.

The most important ergonomic element is weight. However, weight in and of itself is not meaningful without knowing how that weight is distributed. The farther a weight is held from the body, the more exertion is required to hold that weight. The ideal shelf reader should therefore consist of a hand-held wand that has an antenna for shelf scanning at the top while the base is held close to the operator's body. As much as possible, the weight of the wand should be focused at the base. If a wand-style reader is not available, total weight becomes even more crucial since the reader will need to be held away from the operator's body. A wand-style reader recommended for weight distribution

Figure 3.26. Shelf-reading wand.

purposes should, depending on its length, allow the operator to reach everywhere needed without stretching, reaching, or bending.

"Easy on the eyes" is another important ergonomic aspect of a shelf-reading system. Its importance, however, varies depending on the specific application that is being used. A simple inventory requires little by way of screen reading or manual data input. Other applications, such as search and identifying of misplaced materials, generally involve regular stops and starts with the operator going back and forth between scanning shelves and checking to see what appears on the monitor. Obviously, from this perspective (pun intended), the larger the viewing area, the better. Additionally, the viewing area can be no bigger than the device itself. An all-in-one hand-held device, by design, must miniaturize as much as possible. Therefore, for this reason, if not for others, a monitor separated from the reader itself may be preferable. As we noted earlier, the preferred application of some vendors requires the power of a laptop computer to achieve its num-ber-crunching operations. The larger screen of a laptop, as opposed to that available in a PDA-type device, is an added ergonomic by-product.

Power source.

The shelf reader must have sufficient power to read accurately and quickly and do so for sustained periods of time without interruption. Ideally, the reader should be able to operate with no diminishing of performance for a full workday, 8 hours, without recharging. Libraries should request evidence that a particular vendor's reader can oper-ate in real-world conditions for whatever period of time it claims. One approach is to power the device directly from an electrical wall outlet. However, pulling an electrical extension cord through the library may be impractical or even hazardous. If that is the case, a heavy-duty battery may be called for. The kind of heavy-duty battery needed is going to be just that—heavy. Because of weight and size, it will need to travel on a cart. If a cart is required for other purposes—to hold a laptop or RFID coupler—the battery just comes along for the ride.

It is also important to consider what other equipment may be needed when a shelf-reading application is to be used. For example, if doing a search for missing materials, what will the operator do with an item that is found in a wrong location? If weeding the collection using the search application, what will the operator do with items that should be removed from shelves? If identifying mis-shelved materials, what will the opera-tor do with the hand-held device while moving items from one side of the shelf to the other? In many cases, the answer to all these questions is one and the same—some sort of carrier or cart must accompany the operator to hold materials pulled from shelves or to hold the reader itself.

Other features and considerations.

RFID shelf-reading systems may come with a variety of bells and whistles, the value of which will vary with each library. Some vendors offer complete inventory reporting software. Where available, most libraries will prefer to use the inventory utilities that are part of their ILS. Some reports, such as a list of items found or not found during a search, however, must come from the RFID system itself. From a hardware perspec-tive, wireless functionality may be useful in some libraries and applications. However, libraries will find that many shelf-reading applications work best when information is downloaded from the ILS to the reader in batch and then uploaded to the ILS in batch once the activity is completed.

As with all applications, librarians need to understand not only the power of RFID but also its limitations. In that light, it is important that the human element always be considered. Machines work consistently; people do not. How the operator holds the reader and how quickly the reader is passed along shelves will vary constantly. Libraries should therefore consider making a "double-pass" standard shelf-reading procedure. Ideal shelf-reading software, including that used for identifying mis-shelved materials, should work equally well regardless of whether the operator scans shelves in call number order or the reverse.

The major technology limitation, not surprisingly, applies to AV materials. Simply stated, the RFID shelf reader does not provide accurate results when used with CDs and DVDs lined up on a shelf. Best results will be achieved when, instead of using donut-style hub tags on disks themselves, standard book tags are placed in the bottom corners of cases near the spines. But even then, the metal content of disks is likely to inhibit performance. Accurate reading requires pulling each CD and DVD away from shelves so that the reader can face the tag directly.

The reader/ILS interface.

To maximize the number of libraries that can take advantage of RFID technology, vendors need a way for their equipment to operate, regardless of the ILS system the library employs. Creating RFID readers compatible with multiple ILS systems requires a common language that allows RFID equipment to hold an electronic dialog with ILS system's database, where the key data about the library materials is stored. The conversation enables some important features: interoperability, security of private information, minimization of memory requirements for RFID tags, and limiting data duplication. Special software, sometimes called middleware, is used to make the connection between RFID readers and the library's ILS. The middleware provides the ability to translate information captured about materials using RFID readers into data that can be read by the ILS. The software also contains the protocol that handles moving the data electronically from the reader to the ILS.

Data captured by RFID readers has to be written in a specific format that the ILS can recognize. In order to provide information remotely (at a self check-out station, at a security gate, at a book drop, etc.), the remote software must be able to understand the data sent by the ILS. The middleware reads, writes, and transmits properly formatted data allowing the ILS and the remote stations to hold a two-way conversation. The most commonly used format supported by reader-based software and ILS systems is SIP2, developed by the 3M Corporation. Many vendors support the SIP2 specification. There are other specifications, such as SIP (or SIP1), the previous generation specification, and NCIP. The specifications vary, but they all have the same function, to lay out how data must be formatted in order for applications to understand it. Standards for SIP2 are not firm. Each vendor has its variations, but generally the specifications are consistent, especially on the self-service side of the communications.

In order to maintain patron privacy, it is highly recommended that libraries do not store information on RFID tags that can reveal personal data, including book titles, patron addresses, and other information. As we discussed in Chapter 2, minimizing the amount of data on the tag defeats the ability for data thieves to gain personal information by reading tags. However, inside the library, data is needed at the remote points such as self check-out stations. Because of the middleware, the information is available internally, so when data is required by the library or its patrons, it is accessible in a controlled, secure way.

The minimization of data on the tag has an additional benefit. Tags can be kept small and can maintain memory requirements that do not add to either the size or the power requirements for the chips. This allows limits to the tags' range, which, as we have stated before, is a good thing for library implementations. It also keeps tags from growing in size and becoming more intrusive to materials. (In future, tag sizes will probably decrease, even with extended memory capabilities.)

If data on the RFID tag is limited to only key identifiers, data does not have to be duplicated remotely. All data can be centrally stored in the ILS. This eliminates the possibility that data will not be synchronized between the ILS and the RFID tags. Suppose a library chose to store bibliographical information on an RFID tag. When programming an item for the first time, that data would have to be stored both in the ILS and in the tag. If the ILS should become unavailable during the process of adding a new item, it is possible that the data on the tag would not be in sync with the data in the ILS. This creates a maintenance problem. If the data is only stored in the ILS, and the middleware interface handles the communication of this data to a remote station, no synchronization problems can occur.

Using an ILS software-independent model provides libraries flexibility. With that flexibility comes additional decision making. When libraries consider RFID vendors, they should pay attention to the vendor's interface capabilities, to be sure that the protocols supported by the ILS are also supported by the vendor.

3.3 SUMMARY

Now that we have discussed about the tags, hardware, and software used in RFID technology, it is time to use the knowledge gained here to intelligently investigate the purchase of a system. The next chapter covers an introduction to RFID vendors and the questions you will want to ask them.

REFERENCES

American Library Association. (2005). *Guidelines for implementing RFID technologies in libraries: Privacy and intellectual freedom concerns.* Retrieved March 2, 2006, from http://www.ala.org/ala/oif/oifprograms/openhearings/relatedlinksabc/draftrfidguidelines.htm

Chachra, V. (2005, June). *RFID technology in libraries: meet with experts.* Paper presented at the annual conference of the American Library Association, Chicago, IL.

Chachra, V., & McPherson, D (2003, October). *Personal privacy and use of RFID technology in libraries.* Retrieved March 2, 2006, from http://ww.vtls.com/documents/privacy.pdf

Finkenzeller, K. (2003). RFID handbook: *Fundamentals and applications in contactless smart cards and identification* (2nd ed.). West Sussex, England: Wiley.

Heinrich, C. (2005). RFID and beyond: *Growing your business through Real World Awareness.* Indianapolis, IN: Wiley Publishing.

Sweeney, P. J., II. (2005). *RFID for dummies.* Indianapolis, IN: Wiley Publishing.

Chapter 4

How to Select a Vendor

4.1 GATHERING DATA

Several characteristics determine the viability of an RFID vendor. A vendor should have a good track record in providing products and services to libraries. A good track record means they have a solid customer base, have been providing RFID products and services for a number of years, and have a history of completing installations on time and on budget.

A vendor must be financially stable and thus able to fund research and development. A vendor must have the expertise to provide customized solutions as well as solve any problems that may arise.

A vendor must be able to demonstrate a working product for all required applications. A vendor should provide products that meet or exceed industry standards.

A vendor needs to have established working relationships with vendors of integrated library systems (ILS). For example, SirsiDynix Corporation has a certification program that guarantees that they have a working relationship with a given vendor.

When comparing vendors, look at the number and frequency of recent installations in libraries, the company revenue/profit figures, and the number of years they have been offering RFID products. At American Library Association conventions, stop by RFID vendor booths to meet people in the company, view their products, and ask some of the questions cited below. When you have narrowed down the vendors to three, then you should schedule visits to your library from each vendor to present their products to library staff members. During these presentations, vendors can view your library situation and discuss the best solutions for implementing RFID. After meeting each vendor, call and/or visit other libraries that use each vendor.

During the vendor selection process, it is important to interview a variety of vendors and their customers. To prepare for these interviews, take the time to read about RFID issues, both in libraries and in other industries:

RFID in libraries blog   http://libraryrfid.net/wordpress
RFID journal   www.RFIDjournal.com
RFID listerv   RFID_LIB@listproc.sjsu.edu

4.1.1 Current RFID Vendors for Libraries

Current RFID vendors for libraries include

3M http://solutions.3m.com
Bibliotheca http://www.bibliotheca-rfid.com
Checkpoint http://www.checkpointsystems.com
IDSystems http://id-systems.com
Integrated Technology Group www.integratedtek.com
Libramation http://www.libramation.com
Library Automation Technologies http://www.latcorp.com
ST LogiTrack http://www.stlogitrack.com
Tech Logic Corp. http://www.tech-logic.com

4.1.2 Sample Questions to Ask Prospective Vendors

General.

1. How long have you been offering RFID?
2. What ILS vendors does your system work with?
3. How does your system work?
4. How does security work?
5. Is SIP2 required?
6. Do you work with any third-party vendors?
7. Are you certified with our ILS vendor?
8. What libraries are currently using your RFID products?
9. What are the newest developments and/or trends in RFID in libraries?
10. What changes in facilities will be needed to implement RFID?

Tags.

1. What kind of tags do you use?
2. Do the tags meet current standards?
3. What kind of information is stored on the tag?
4. How are tags programmed?
5. How fragile are the tags?
6. Can the tags work with other vendors?
7. Do the tags need a cover label?
8. Can the tags themselves be imprinted?

Tagging.

1. How are tags programmed?
2. What equipment is required for tagging?

3. What materials can be tagged?
4. Can all materials be tagged on the item itself (not just the container)?
5. Do you have statistics on tagging rates?

Security.

1. Can security cameras be used to capture an alarm event?
2. How is security turned on and off with your system?
3. Does security work equally with all applications?

Check out.

1. What equipment is required at the circulation desk?
2. Does your system provide multiple-item check out?

Self check-out.

1. Do you offer self check-out stations?
2. What equipment is required?
3. Is multiple-item check out available?
4. Is there remote monitoring capability at self check-out stations?

Sorting.

1. Do you offer automated sorting?
2. What equipment is required?
3. Will the sorting system accept all materials? (Provide a list of types of library materials.)

Inventory control.

1. Do you offer inventory control?
2. What equipment is required for inventory control?
3. Describe the process of inventory control.

Implementation.

1. Please detail the implementation process.
2. Who supplies software? Hardware? Tags?
3. Who does installation of software? Of hardware? Of sorting? Of security gates?
4. Do you provide training? Is it at an extra cost?
5. What kind of support do you offer?
6. How do you characterize your customer service?

Maintenance.

1. Do you offer a maintenance agreement for ongoing support?
2. Does your maintenance agreement detail response time and a schedule of updates?
3. Do you offer any warranties?
4. Can you provide estimated costs?

4.1.3 Sample Questions to Ask Customers of Each Vendor

General.

1. Has your vendor provided any solutions or special service?
2. Do you utilize multiple-item check out at self check-out stations? At the circulation desk? At check in? Why or why not?
3. Do you offer automated check in at book drops?
4. Did the vendor work well with your ILS vendor?

Tags.

1. Have you had problems with your tags?
2. Do they seem to be holding up?

Tagging.

1. Has your vendor provided any solutions or special service?
2. Is the tagging process easy?
3. Did you calculate a tagging rate?
4. Who does your tagging?

Security.

1. How well does security work at the security gates?
2. What is the false-alarm frequency? Do the gates fail to go off at times?
3. Do you use additional security devices such as Kwik cases for CDs and DVDs?

Check out.

1. Does the RFID check-out process save time?
2. Do your staff members experience any problems with check out?

Self check-out.

1. How patron friendly is the self check-out station?
2. How well does security turn on/off at the self check-out stations?
3. Do your patrons like using self check-out stations?
4. What percentage of your circulation is from self check-out stations?
5. What kinds of problems do you have with self check-out stations?
6. Do you integrate credit-card payments at self check-out stations?
7. If you use security cases for CDs and DVDs, do you have release mechanisms built-in?

Sorting.

1. How well does security turn on/off with sorting equipment?
2. Do any of your materials get damaged from sorting?
3. What kinds of problems do you have with your sorting system?
4. Has sorting provided a solution/benefit to your library?

Inventory control.

1. How do you use inventory control?
2. Does it meet your expectations?

Implementation.

1. How did you conduct your RFID conversion project?
2. How large is your collection?
3. How long did it take you to convert to RFID?
4. Describe the vendor's training program.
5. How did your installation go?
6. Are you satisfied with the products?
7. Is there anything you wish you had done differently?
8. Are you satisfied with the customer service you receive?
9. Was your implementation experience close to your expectations?

Maintenance.

1. What has been the response time by the vendor when problems arise?
2. Are you satisfied with the customer support?
3. How often do you receive software updates?
4. What kind of maintenance agreement do you have?
5. Is there one component that is more troublesome than other components?
6. What types of maintenance have you had to do on your equipment?
7. What is the average turn-around time for getting replacement parts?

Return on investment.

1. Have you realized a return on your investment?
2. If not, when do you hope to realize a return on your investment?
3. How have your staffing levels changed after implementing RFID?
4. Have there been any unexpected results from implementing RFID?
5. Were there any hidden costs?
6. Has library service improved with the addition of RFID?

4.1.4   Questions to Discuss at Your Library

1. Is RFID right for us at this time?
2. What do we hope to accomplish using RFID?
3. What are our priorities?
4. What will an RFID system cost? Can we afford it?
5. Will we need a dual mode system that supports both bar codes and RFID tags?
6. Can we afford to tag all items or should we phase in RFID?
7. Who will do our tagging?
8. Will we have a budget for RFID conversion or will existing staff do the conversion?
9. What characteristics are most important in choosing an RFID vendor?
10. What vendor will best fit our needs?

4.2   DETERMINING APPROACH

There are several approaches to take in selecting a vendor. While keeping in mind the data that has been gathered, you can determine which approach to take.

One approach is to select a vendor for each component of an RFID implementation. With this approach, you can select the vendor who best meets your needs for each component. For example, you may select one vendor for tags, readers, and software; another vendor for sorting equipment; and another vendor for self check-out stations. This approach gives you control over each aspect of an RFID implementation. You are not committed to only one vendor, which allows for changing vendors in the future as technology changes. The disadvantages of this approach include finding vendors who will work well together, having the knowledge, confidence, and time to oversee the RFID implementation; and communicating and coordinating with several vendors.

A second approach is to select one vendor who will provide all aspects of an RFID implementation. A single vendor will select other vendors to supply components that they do not normally provide. For example, Warren-Newport Public Library had one vendor (Integrated Technology Group) install their RFID system. This vendor provided the entire RFID solution for the library. ITG partnered with Tagsys, which supplied the tags, readers, and gates, and with FKI Logistics, which supplied the sorting system. With the one-vendor approach, that vendor has responsibility for all aspects of the RFID implementation. There is only one vendor to deal with. The disadvantages of this approach include lack of choice in products and vendors involved in the implementation, lack of direct communication with the various vendors, and the inability to change vendors later as new options or developments in RFID occur.

A third approach involves hiring an outside person to manage the RFID implementation. This person would have the expertise to determine the needs of the library and then select the most appropriate vendors and products. This person would oversee the entire process. This approach allows for maintaining control in the selection of vendors, but this approach can be costlier.

4.3   WRITING THE RFP

The request for proposal (RFP) process can help you obtain the right vendor and services that your library requires. There are many different ways to go about writing an RFP. Some libraries, in lieu of the RFP process, just obtain cost estimates and project details from a few vendors who offer unique systems. The advantage to this approach is that you do not have to understand a vendor's products and services in detail, which you would need to write and submit an RFP. You can let the vendors detail what their products and services are and then evaluate which vendor's approach will be the best solution for the library.

Other libraries prepare an RFP, which does force you to be specific about your needs and requirements. Generally, an RFP must contain details regarding all general and technical requirements, including hardware, software, tags, readers, security gates, inventory wands, book-drop readers, conveyors, sorters, workstations, self-check stations, and conversion stations. The RFP should request detailed price quotes for all the above items, along with additional costs such as existing equipment upgrades, training costs, costs for documentation, licensing costs, and maintenance costs.

The RFP should address whether a vendor provides a complete chain of products, or other vendors will be providing some products. The RFP will specify applicable standards as well as project expectations, budget, and timelines. It should cover expectations for customer service, technical services, and ongoing support as problems arise. The RFP should request warranty information, maintenance-contract language, and the availability of reward programs or other incentives. Finally, the RFP should request information on how future products will be implemented. An example RFP is included in the appendix.

4.4 EVALUATING PROPOSALS

After receiving proposals, you must now weigh all the information that you have gathered to determine which vendor is the best for your library. Cost alone should not be the sole criteria for selecting a vendor. Out of the qualifying vendors who will provide a working product within a price range that is acceptable, which vendor will be a fit with your organization? Which vendor impressed you with their knowledge and experience? Which vendor had the best feedback from existing customers? Selecting the best vendor takes time and thoughtful consideration, but the rewards are great when you have selected a vendor who will be responsive to your needs and will assure a successful project.

Chapter 5

How to Manage the RFID Conversion Project

5.1   ORDERING TAGS AND WEEDING

When the RFID contract is signed, it is time to order the equipment and tags that will be needed to convert the existing collection to RFID and to begin tagging new materials. Before beginning tagging, complete a thorough weeding of all collections. Run statistics on the various collection sizes. Approximate how many items will need to be tagged and add the number of items that are added to the collection annually to calculate the number of tags needed for the first year. If you are using more than one type of tag, then you have to calculate the number of items for each type of tag. For example, if you plan to tag DVDs and CDs, then you must calculate the number of circular tags that will be needed for those materials. Unlike magnetic strips, which only concern security, RFID tags are required on all items that circulate. Many libraries that omit magnetic strips on some types of materials, such as audio books that are not high-theft items, must now include those materials with RFID in order to use self-check stations for all materials and/or to implement sorting. With RFID, it is necessary to tag everything that circulates, since the tag provides both the bar code as well as security.

Since it is possible to use both bar codes and RFID tags at the same time, libraries can phase in the tagging of some areas of the collection. For example, items on a book-mobile, items at a branch, or magazines may be tagged at a later date. However, these items can neither be checked out at a self-check station, nor can they be checked in using RFID sorting or book drop automated check in. If the funds are available to tag all items, then be sure to include the number of magazine issues currently held and expected during the first year in your calculations for number of tags needed.

5.2 TAG PLACEMENT

It is also necessary to determine where the tags should be placed in your materials when determining the number of tags needed. Your vendor may have suggestions regarding tag placement. For books, tags need to be located near the spine of the book to allow for optimum use of an inventory wand. Tags are placed in the lower left quadrant of the back cover close to the spine, but not in the hinge area, which can damage the tag. A discussion of cover labels follows this section.

Tags should be somewhat staggered when placed in books to optimize reading of the tags. Therefore, varying the placement of a tag by quarter of an inch is recommended as you tag books that are sitting side by side.

When a book has a dust jacket, the tag is placed underneath the dust jacket and is turned sideways to allow the bar code to be scanned.

Tags for children's board books are placed inside the back cover in a spot that does not cover an illustration or text. Putting the tag on the outside of the book should be avoided as it leaves the tag exposed to damage from book drops.

Figure 5.1. Placement of square RFID tag in book.

Figure 5.2. Staggered placement of square RFID tags in books.

Books that have accompanying cassettes or CDs and circulate in bags are also tagged in the way just described.

Videocassettes are tagged using square tags that are placed on one of the windows of the videocassette. Though tags could be placed on the center of the videocassette, the tag would cover the videocassette title. Tags placed on the videocassette windows adhere very well and do not seem to cause problems with videocassette players.

Figure 5.3. Placement of square RFID tag in book with dust jacket.

Figure 5.4.   Example of board book.

Figure 5.5.   Placement of square RFID tag in board book.

Figure 5.6. Placement of cover label over RFID tag in board book.

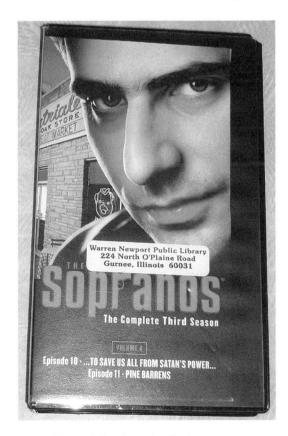

Figure 5.7. Example of videocassette.

Figure 5.8. Placement of RFID tag on window of videocassette.

Books on cassette and CD are tagged with only one RFID tag, even though there may be many cassettes or CDs in the set. Books on cassette and CD are not considered to be high-theft items. Square tags are placed under the cover material that is inserted into the storage case or container.

There is no need to place a cover label over the square tag, because it is protected by the insert. However, a cover label with a bar code is placed on the back of the insert, which can then be scanned when necessary.

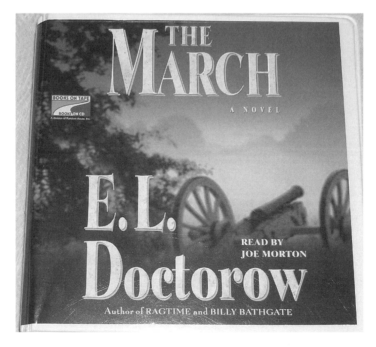

Figure 5.9. Example of book on CD.

Figure 5.10. Placement of RFID tag on container insert of book on CD.

Individual CDs are tagged with a circular tag that is placed on the disc itself. A special device is used to place the circular tag on the CD. This device consists of a spindle on a platform, which is the exact size of the hole in the center of the CD. The circular tag is placed over the spindle and onto the CD. A cover label is then placed over the tag.

As with all items using a circular tag, a bar code is placed on the outside of the item, since the cover label is too small to include a bar code that can be scanned.

Individual DVDs are tagged in the same way as the individual CDs, with a circular tag that is placed on the disc itself. Again, the same spindle device is used to assure even placement of the tag. Multiple DVDs that come in a set, such as a season of television programs, are tagged with just one tag, which is usually placed on the last DVD in the set. If a patron returns the set but leaves the last DVD in DVD player, the item will not check in. With sorting, the item goes in a "problem" bin of items that are handled individually. The clerk will examine the item for a missing tag, will check the item in manually, and will call the patron to bring in the missing DVD. One of the changes as a result of implementing sorting is that staff members no longer check each set for missing parts. The time that it takes to stop and open each item is not feasible in relation to the infrequent occurrences of missing items. It is up to patrons to check for missing parts both at self-check stations and at staff-assisted check-out stations. Each multipart item has a special label that clearly states the number and types of parts contained in the item.

Figure 5.11. Placement of cover label for a book on CD.

Figure 5.12. Example of CD.

Figure 5.13. CD is placed on the tagging device.

Figure 5.14. RFID circular tag is placed on the CD using the device.

Figure 5.15.   Cover label is placed over the tag on the CD using the device.

Figure 5.16.   Placement of bar code on outside of CD.

Figure 5.17.   Example of magazine.

Figure 5.18.   Placement of tag and cover label inside magazine cover.

Staff members no longer need to open each item, thus reducing one of the triggers for carpal tunnel syndrome.

Magazines are tagged using square tags that are placed on the first page inside the cover.

5.3 BAR CODES AND COVER LABELS

Another consideration is the need for bar codes and cover labels. Cover labels are needed to protect the tag. It may be advisable to have bar codes printed on the cover labels for new materials. Printed bar codes are helpful for identifying items at work-stations that do not have readers, such as throughout a technical services department that is already equipped with bar-code scanners. Staff members doing acquisitions and cataloging find it easiest to scan a bar code to determine what copy they have in hand. It helps increase efficiency and accuracy by scanning bar codes instead of typing in bar-code numbers. Public libraries that buy multiple copies will also benefit from having bar codes on all items, which eases the task of identifying which copy you have in hand without needing a reader. Printed bar codes are also helpful for inter-library loan, when other libraries without RFID need to identify an item. Printed bar codes are also necessary if not every branch or bookmobile has been converted to RFID, thus allowing a dual system to be functional. Bar codes that are printed on the label that covers the RFID tag may also include the library logo, address, phone and fax numbers, and Web site address. Some vendors will provide the printed labels. You just need to submit a photo ready copy of the design along with the bar-code range. Be sure to send the beginning bar-code number that does not duplicate any printed bar codes that you may still be using. When getting set up, your vendor will require the specifications for the type of bar code that you use, the number of digits, and so on.

You will need two types of cover labels for each type of tag—one type to cover the tags for conversion items (no bar code, assuming they already have bar codes on them) and one type to cover the tags for new materials (with a bar code). For example, if your library uses two types of tags (square and circular), then you will need four types of cover labels. The circular cover labels, because of their small size, come imprinted with the library name and a small eye-readable bar code. Again, as you approximate the number of tags needed for each type of material, you will need to approximate the number of labels you will need with bar codes and without bar codes. Be sure to calculate the bar-code ranges necessary for each collection, avoiding overlap of any bar-code numbers.

5.4 EQUIPMENT FOR TAGGING

To tag a collection, you will need tagging stations, which are comprised of a reader, a computer with tagging program software, and a bar-code scanner. You will eventually have a computer workstation in technical services that is dedicated to tagging new materials, but during the conversion process, it is more efficient to have portable tagging stations.

Portable tagging stations can be used to tag materials right in the stacks which is more efficient than moving the materials to a permanent workstation. Inexpensive utility carts on wheels can be used to hold the tagging station equipment as you move through the stacks.

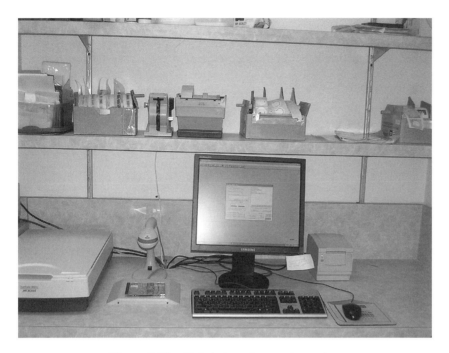

Figure 5.19. Technical services tagging station.

Figure 5.20. Utility cart on wheels for tagging in the stacks.

The readers that you purchase for the library can be used temporarily as tagging stations during the conversion process. Laptop computers are ideal for portable tagging stations. Many vendors will offer a rental program to rent laptop computers. Long-life batteries are recommended for the laptops, along with extension cords, which will allow for uninterrupted tagging in the stacks. Finally, you will need to determine a place to plug-in and recharge the laptops. It is helpful to note the time with a post-it note when a laptop is plugged-in, so that staff members can readily determine which laptop is ready for the next team of tagging staff.

5.5   STAFFING CONSIDERATIONS

Determining the staff hours needed to tag a collection is dependent on many factors: the size of the collection (after weeding), the percentage of audio-visual materials (which take longer to tag), and the number of portable tagging stations. Tagging rates vary among individuals, but on average, items can be tagged at the rate of 50 per hour (books are faster than AV). If two people tag at one tagging station, the rate can be increased somewhat as two people divide the tasks:

- Pull the book off the shelf.
- Open the book.
- Place the tag in the book. ◄───────
- Place a cover label over the tag. ◄

  > It is possible to combine these two steps by placing the cover label over the tag and then inserting the tag in the item.

- Scan the existing bar code.
- Place the book on the reader.
- Program the tag.
- Mark the item on the outside (i.e., check mark on existing bar code).
- Place the book back on the shelf.

Therefore, 200,000 items will take approximately 4,000 hours to tag. If you have six portable tagging stations, then the project will take forty-eight 8-hour days, 5 days a week, with all laptops in use at all times, or about 16 weeks. If it is difficult to staff the project consistently, you will need to add roughly another 8 weeks to complete the tagging. Many libraries have used volunteers of all ages to do tagging. This will increase the time it takes to tag the collection, as volunteers come when they are able, and it takes time to train the number of volunteers needed to complete the project.

Some libraries require existing staff to do the tagging. This practice gets staff involved in the project. There is no outright cost in having existing staff do the tagging, but the loss of time doing regular job requirements can be cumulative and significant. For example, if a technical services department takes on tagging all audio-visual materials, a backlog can develop in cataloging and processing new materials.

Some libraries hire special staff to do the tagging. It is possible to offer a minimum wage rate for tagging. A library can hire a team of people to work half days to get the tagging project completed. This approach has a cost, but a team of trained people can work efficiently and steadily to get the project completed.

Some libraries use a combination of all the above approaches. Warren-Newport Public Library used volunteers, all staff members, and paid workers for a brief time. It took 6 months to tag 200,000 items. Around 100 volunteers tagged during mostly daytime hours. All staff members were required to tag five shelves. The technical services department tagged most of the audio-visual materials. Paid temporary workers began tagging during the last 2 months to assure that the project was completed on schedule. Students learned tagging very easily. Many students without jobs tagged during the summer months, earning a recommendation from the library for future jobs and/or fulfilling school volunteer project requirements.

5.6   TRAINING STAFF

When you have made a decision on how to staff the project, and the equipment and tags have arrived, then it is time to plan how to train everyone who will be tagging. When working with large numbers of people and/or working over many hours daily, it is best to train many people to do the training. Additionally, it is best to provide written procedures that stay with every mobile workstation so a person tagging can review them when necessary.

Training should include the following:

- Orientation to project—why we are doing it, what it entails
- How to tag books including step-by-step instructions and hands-on practice
- How to tag audio-visual materials for experienced workers
- Operation of equipment including laptop, software, reader, and bar-code scanner
- Placement of tags and the importance of staggering tags
- Precautions such as keeping tags and readers 3 feet apart to avoid programming all tags with one bar code; do not use tags marked as "bad" tags (one library had tagging staff stand between the two, with tags on a book cart and the reader on a media cart)
- Trouble shooting if tag does not write; making sure tag is over the reader; what to do if tag fails to write (give to person in charge)
- Procedures for keeping track of what parts of the collection are done, such as signing in and out in a collection notebook; noting dates, names, call numbers of items, and time spent is an efficient way to monitor project status and to spot-check an individual's work

Date	Name	600s Begin	End	Hours
6/1/03	Jane Doe	600 ADE	612.1 TAR	2
6/2/03	John Smith	612.1 TAR	616.81 GOR	3
6/4/03	Jane Doe	616.81 GOR	621.382 NOL	2.5
		Adult Fiction		
7/1/03	Alice Smith	F ADE	F COR	3.5
7/2/03	Jim Doe	F COR	F EDD	2
7/3/03	Alice Smith	F EDD	F HAR	1.75

Figure 5.21.

5.7 TAGGING NEW MATERIALS

As you begin the conversion project, you need to also begin tagging new materials. You need to determine who will do the tagging, where they will do the tagging, and when they will do the tagging. Some libraries do tagging at the beginning of the workflow, as materials are unpacked. Others clip or tape the cover label to the item and have the tagging occur during processing, the final phase of the workflow. Warren-Newport Public Library has volunteers tag most new materials right after they are unpacked, before they are received and linked to the catalog record. However, since many AV materials are not in their final packaging, AV items are tagged during processing by staff members. It is handy to have an apparatus for dispensing tags and labels. Dispensers are available commercially, or they can be made from cardboard boxes.

5.8 FIRST PASS-THROUGH

As the tagging conversion begins, you will need a method of marking items that have been tagged, so they can be readily identified as the project progresses. As items are tagged, staff can mark an outside bar code with a small check mark to identify that the item has a tag, or staff can put a dot in a consistent, visible place using a permanent marker such as on the spine or on top of the pages.

It will save time later when you are trying to catch items that do not have a tag. If you implement sorting, then items without a tag will be identified during the check-in process by being sorted into a "problem" bin. However, if an item does not get checked out, then you still need a way of easily identifying it on the shelf as not having been tagged.

Figure 5.22. Marking items that have a tag.

Figure 5.23.   Marking items that have a tag.

5.9   SECOND PASS-THROUGH

When the entire collection has been passed through once and tags have been placed in all items on the shelf, then it is time to do a second pass-through. At this time, all items being returned to circulation without a tag need to be identified and tagged before shelving. Either items needing tags can be delivered to a tagging station, or a mobile station can be placed in the returns area to tag items as they are returned. As tagging

Figure 5.24.   Marking items that have a tag.

staff members pass through the shelves again, they can quickly determine whether an item needs a tag by examining the spine for a dot or by tipping out the item to look for a check mark.

5.10 PROBLEM MATERIALS

Some items will be difficult to tag because of the presence of metallic material in the dust jacket of a book, in the cover of a paperback book, or in the CD or DVD itself. A damaged tag could also be the reason why the tag does not write. Materials with problems are then referred to an experienced staff person. Luckily, these occurrences are rare.

Trouble shooting an item that is difficult to tag involves running through a series of tasks to fix the problem. First, place the item on a reader and click on "quick read" to see what the tag has on it. The tag must be completely over the reader to be written. Try writing the tag again. If it still does not write, then try removing the dust jacket and see if it will write. If it writes without the dust jacket, then try to read it with the dust jacket. If it does not read with the dust jacket, then either remove the dust jacket permanently or use a scanner in the department to scan the dust jacket and make a new one. The new jacket is then printed out on a color printer and inserted into the dust-jacket cover.

If the cover of a paperback book has metallic material in it and the tag does not write, go through the steps already mentioned to see whether the tag will write. Next, remove the tag that does not write and place a tag, without adhering it, inside the book to see if it will write. If it writes, then adhere the tag in the book. If it does not write, then make a "sandwich" tag.

You will need the following materials to make a sandwich tag: a cutting tool to cut a template out of cardboard, and a piece of cardboard.

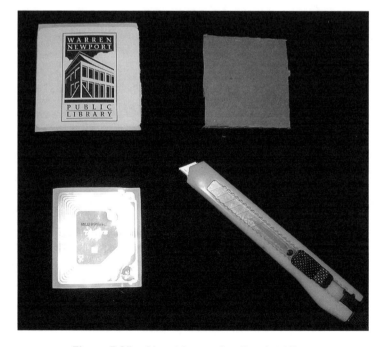

Figure 5.25. Materials to make a "sandwich" tag.

The following title contained metallic material and the tag would not write.

First cut a piece of cardboard that is slightly smaller than the square tag. Next cut a square hole in the back cover of the book using the cardboard template.

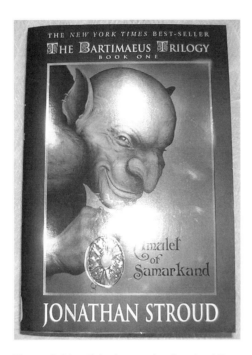

Figure 5.26. Title that needs a "sandwich" tag.

Figure 5.27.

Place a cover label without a bar code over the square hole on the back of the book.

Figure 5.28.

On the inside of the back cover, place a square tag over the square hole.

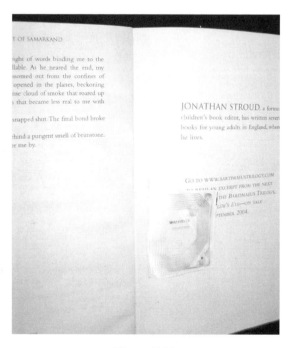

Figure 5.29.

Place a bar code cover label over the square tag on the inside cover of the book and program the tag.

Figure 5.30.

As a final step, reinforce the sandwich tag with book tape on both sides.

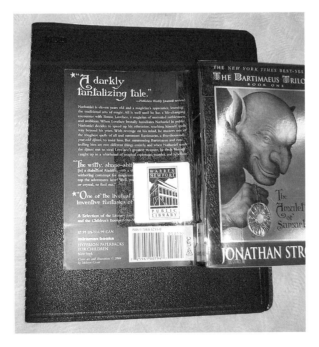

Figure 5.31.

When a CD or DVD does not write, try to remove the circular tag carefully and try to program the tag by itself. If the tag writes successfully, place the tag on the item and click on "quick read" to see if the tag will read. If the tag still does not read, then you may have to tag the case with a square tag placed in a lower corner. If the existing circular tag does not write successfully by itself, then use a new tag and follow the aforementioned steps.

5.11   PROJECT EVALUATION

When the second pass is completed, tagging will still need to continue for items being returned to the library. Most of the collection will be tagged and it is possible to calculate the cost of the RFID conversion. Using the data that has been collected, including the hours spent tagging, the size of the collection, and any salaries paid, you can calculate the rate of tagging and the costs. A project evaluation should also include what worked and what did not work. Broward County Library in Florida provided an online account of their RFID project. It is found at http://www.tech-logic.com/browardco/default.htm.

5.12   GOING LIVE

Any new system will work better if there is library employee buy-in. Employees need to be kept apprised of the plans and they need to have all their questions answered. It is essential to elicit their input on how a system will be implemented. It is important to reassure employees that their jobs will not be lost. Employees need to understand what changes to expect and why these changes are occurring.

Training should be organized for circulation, technical services, and for all other staff. Staff members need time to practice with new equipment and procedures until they feel comfortable.

You must also plan on how to introduce the new system to customers. It is helpful to notify customers that a new and improved system is coming. Staff members should be trained on how to assist customers at self-check stations. Self-check use is higher when customers have a good experience using it the first time. For this reason, it is preferable to have a staff person at or near self-check stations to provide customer orientation to RFID.

With these considerations, you can plan your "go live" schedule and specify the date you switch over to RFID.

Appendix A

Answers to Frequently Asked Questions

The impetus for writing this book came out of the presentations that the authors have organized and participated in on the subject of RFID technology at various library conferences and workshops. The many questions and concerns that audiences raised during these presentations made the need for such a book obvious. Once we embarked upon the process, we also consulted colleague librarians from around the world via e-mail or telephone. While many of the issues are addressed in the core of the book, we have chosen to address others in this appendix. We consider some matters to be of such import that we deal with them both in the core of the book and here as well.

A.1 GENERAL

What are the differences between bar-code-based systems and RFID technology?

Perhaps the biggest difference is that the bar code needs a line of sight, whereas RFID does not. This feature of RFID saves item process time in libraries in four areas: check out, return of items, sorting, and inventory control. For example, in the past, a Vatican Library inventory process would have taken a month. When the RFID system is fully implemented, this task will take only a few hours (Vatican Library employs RFID tracking, 2004). In another example, a bar-code library that is using an automatic book-drop system has to put bar codes on both sides of an item; that is, an additional bar code needs to be added onto each item, because a bar-code scanner has to see the bar code to read it. An RFID library that is using an automatic book-drop system does not require additional process, because the RFID tag can be read within a reader's range.

How many libraries in the United States are using RFID?

As of December 2005, there were about 300 libraries using RFID in the United States.

Which was the first library in the world to implement RFID?

The first RFID library was the National Library of Singapore.

What is a data model?

A data model defines the requirements for data elements and data structure on the RFID tag. More information regarding the data model is in Chapter 2.

A.2 MIGRATION FROM BAR CODES TO RFID

How do we deal with a mixed RFID/bar-code collection?

This is particularly important for self check-out. The verification procedure used at self-service stations should take into account that some items may not have RFID tags. If an RFID tag is not found, the system should automatically instruct patrons to scan an item's bar code.

Does it make sense for non-RFID libraries to start first with bar-code-based self check-out before moving to RFID-based systems?

If the location of bar codes on materials is relatively consistent, this can certainly be done. Most RFID vendors provide bar-code-based self check-out systems that can be easily upgraded to RFID. Libraries should verify the upgrade cost for hardware and ensure that no additional software need be purchased. If the system has multiple units out in the field, it is important that the system provide a staff person with the ability to configure and make changes to all units connected to the library's network.

What about bar codes for new materials?

As noted, bar codes will continue to be necessary on all items, including those with RFID tags. For existing collections, libraries will want to use plain RFID tags with separate protective overlay labels or RFID tags with a preprinted library logo. For new materials, labels and preprinted tags are both available with sequentially printed bar-code labels, so that additional bar-code labels need not be affixed to materials. However, for system-wide consistency, particularly in those cases where existing bar-code labels are not in the same area where RFID tags are normally placed (inside the back cover near the spine), libraries may decide to continue using separate bar-code labels.

Should RFID tags be placed in all new materials?

Those materials belonging to the RFID branch will have RFID tags. It is strongly recommended that all new materials, including those belonging to other libraries, also be RFID tagged. This, together with an aggressive weeding program, will speed the system-wide migration to RFID. This is all the more true if materials are processed centrally; separate programming stations need not be purchased for each library, and technical service staff can use a single consistent process. This also holds true for any outside book processors that the library system may use.

What are the implications for "holds"?

Libraries considering RFID are generally interested in relieving staff of as many clerical duties as possible. They may have already implemented a self-service holds pickup system or would like to do so. A properly designed self check-out station's ability to handle both RFID and bar-coded materials means that even if the reserved item comes from another library and does not have an RFID tag, the patron can still check it out without assistance. It is preferable, however, that all items in the RFID library, including those that do not belong to it, be RFID tagged. The RFID library may want to RFID tag all items belonging to the system that come its way, including those outside its own collection that temporarily fills a hold. Since a significant number of reserved materials are new, this presents another argument for tagging all of the system's materials with RFID.

What if the RFID library also has an automated materials handling system?

Some automated returns systems handle both RFID and bar-coded materials. In most cases, however, the return checks in only those items with RFID tags. If a sorting system is used, it is important that any item returned without an RFID tag is automatically directed to the sorting unit's "exception" bin for further staff processing.

What about the library's existing electromagnetic (EM) or radio frequency (RF) security systems?

The RFID security system will not detect EM and RF tags. This presents another argument in favor of putting RFID tags in all new items since those are often the most likely to be stolen and requested to fill holds at the RFID library. EM and RF security systems will not detect RFID tags. RFID tags will not interfere with the tags from these other systems. However, RFID tags should not be placed over RF tags or directly opposite them (if, for example, the RF tag was on the outside cover near the spine at the same spot that the RFID would be placed on the inside of the cover). If the library currently places RF tags beneath book pockets, it may choose to implement self check-out using "detuning" receipts that the patron places in the pockets to deactivate security. This special receipt paper would be replaced with standard receipt paper once the system is converted to RFID.

What factors affect the speed of the migration path?

The most critical factor affecting the speed of migration is the tagging of the collection. How fast the library system chooses to tag its collection depends on financial and human resources. Tags must be purchased while RFID-programming stations may be purchased or leased. Some vendors offer programming stations that can also be used for general circulation purposes. This means that equipment purchased for programming can also be used for check out and check in at staff stations. Programming systems that also dispense and/or print tags are limited to those functions only. The library system may choose, therefore, to purchase only a limited number of these units, moving them from one location to the next. Tag-programming systems are also available for lease.

What about library systems with floating collections?

Public library systems with floating collections present a different set of challenges. By floating collection, we mean that no individual library branch owns materials. Wherever an item lands is where it stays until it is requested by another location. The frequency of materials moving between branches will determine how feasible it is to do a branch-by-branch migration. Where movement is frequent, there may be no choice but to convert the entire system to RFID all at the same time.

A.3   PRIVACY

Does RFID endanger patron privacy?

While one can imagine all sorts of extraordinary RFID-enabled measures that someone might take to learn the contents of a library patron's briefcase or book bag, potential invasions of privacy that have nothing do with RFID technology are far simpler and more likely. Libraries should follow ALA Guidelines (American Library Association, 2005) in this regard, storing only a bar-code number on the tag.

Should bibliographic information be programmed into the tag?

No. Author, title, and call number reside in the library's database and are accessible via the RFID tag through its bar-code number. Incorporating this information would, in addition, add complexity to and slow the programming operation. Also, the inclusion of bibliographic information on the tag has the potential for compromising patron privacy.

Should publishers start to embed RFID tags with ISBN (or EPC) in items? Will patron privacy be compromised?

Should this happen (and it is not likely to happen for another 5 years or so, in 2011), patron privacy can still be protected, at least in the library world. Libraries may protect patron privacy in three ways:

1. The ISBN can be deactivated by librarians before the books or AV items are delivered from the department of technical services to the department of circulation. The "kill" command turns off the ISBN permanently, and this process is not reversible, that is, it cannot be reactivated.
2. Should publishers embed rewritable tags in items, librarians may replace the ISBN with a bar-code number, and lock it to prevent rewriting.
3. With password protection built into the RFID tag, only authorized personnel can read and write the tag. The password-protected functionality for ISO 15693 compliant products has been on the market since February 2006 (TI RFID Newsletters, 2005, November/December).

Should patrons, students, and faculty be informed that the library is using RFID technology?

Yes. According to the ALA Guidelines, libraries need to inform patrons of the use of RFID in their libraries. There are federal and state laws and legislation for RFID (see section of Privacy Concerns in Chapter 2). Libraries are advised to be proactive in their communication with their communities, so as to prevent the spreading of misinformation about the technology.

Is RFID technology covered under data security law?

The U.S. law of information technology (IT) security also applies to RFID. The law of IT security covers identity, authenticity, integrity, obligation, and confidentiality.

Do library RFID tags need to be encrypted?

The fact that the item bar-code number is meaningful only once it is associated with the library's database is a form of encryption in and of itself. Encryption increases system complexity and is likely to increase the read/process time. Encryption also comes at the expense of other benefits, most importantly interoperability. Moreover, while encryption may serve to mollify some privacy advocates, it is not likely to satisfy all.

A.4   STANDARDS AND INTEROPERABILITY

Are there recognized standards for RFID tags?

All vendors supply libraries with passive tags operating at the high frequency (HF) of 13.56 MHz. The ISO standard for RFID is 18000-3 standard, into which the standard for noncontact cards ISO 15693 has been incorporated. See the section on tags in Chapter 3 for more detailed information.

Can a reader read tags from different vendors?

The ISO standard for RFID, ISO 18000-3, is a general technology standard, not an application standard specifically designed for libraries. In theory, this means that all tag and reader manufacturers that adhere to the standard will be capable of reading each other's tags. In practice, however, it is important to remember that tags and readers are designed to work together within a matched component system and that full functionality is dependent on this appropriate match. In addition, different vendors use different data structures so that making sense out of data may be more challenging than simply reading.

A.5 TAGS AND TAG PROGRAMMING

What is the difference between a "read/write" (R/W) tag and a "write once, read many" (WORM) tag?

Once a WORM tag is initially written to, the information on the tag can never be changed. WORM tags, therefore, do not have a security bit that is automatically turned off and on as materials are checked out or in; RFID security systems using WORM tags must therefore read the complete item identification (bar code) numbers on the RFID tags and then communicate with a database in order to determine whether an item has been properly checked out or not. R/W tags include a security bit that is turned off and on automatically during circulation processes. While it is recommended that the item ID number be locked, other information that the library may choose to include on the tag may be changed at any time.

When will libraries be able to buy a 5-cent tag?

As tag manufacturing volume increases, prices will continue to fall as they have since RFID was first introduced into libraries. However, since tags used in libraries differ from those used in other applications, the kind of volume necessary to produce a tag for under 10 cents is probably quite far away.

How much do RFID tags cost now?

Prices vary based on the type and quantity of the tag being purchased. As of the date of this book's publication (mid 2006), prices for standard book tags average between 50 and 60 cents each.

How much memory does a library tag need?

At present, library tags range from 64 to 1024 bits (kilobit). The smaller the memory size, the cheaper the cost of manufacturing it. Though the Auto ID Center believes that a 128-bit chip could cover all the items made on earth, the Danish RFID Working Group recommends a chip size of 256 bits (32 bytes). This memory size has more than sufficient room to hold not only the bar-code number but also other nonbibliographic data, such as item type, multipart information, and location.

How long does it take to program a tag?

With most systems, all that is required to program a tag is the scanning of an item's bar code. It therefore takes only a second or two to program a tag. Most of the time needed for conversion consists of placing the tag and if used, overlay in the item.

How long does it take to convert a collection?

The time needed for conversion depends on the number of staff, or volunteers if used, that are assigned to the conversion project and the number of conversion stations purchased or leased from the RFID vendor. Most systems allow a two-person team to convert over four books per minute. Obviously, inclusion of only bar-code numbers on tags makes the process the fastest possible.

Are defective tags likely to be discovered during the conversion process?

The defect rate should be below 2%. Vendors' conversion software notifies users should programming fail. Most vendors guarantee tags for the life of the items to which they are applied.

Are bar codes still needed once a library has completed its conversion to RFID?

Since an eye-readable number is still needed, it makes sense to include a bar code as well. Bar codes are also needed for inter-library loan purposes. For the purpose of programming a tag, the scanning of a bar code is the most accurate and fastest methodology. The Danish RFID Working Group also recommends using a bar code for RFID tag programming.

Should libraries use preprogrammed tags?

Most vendors offer preprogrammed tags. However, since the actual programming of a tag is usually so fast and easy, libraries have not found the additional expense to be justified.

How are the authors' libraries handling AV materials?

The Chicago State University (CSU) Library places standard book tags on the cases of AV materials, not on the discs or videos themselves. CSU's AV items are not open to the public; they are stored in the Automated Retrieving System (ARS). Warren-Newport Public Library (WNPL) uses the "donut" hub tags on CDs and DVDs, tagging the last disc in the case of multipart sets. Valuable discs are kept in locking cases that have the capability of being opened by patrons at the self check-out following a successful check out. CSU places standard book tags on video cases while WNPL places standard tags directly on videocassettes. In neither library are individual audiocassettes tagged; a single tag on an audio book is used.

How do the authors' libraries handle individual serial issues?

CSU tags each serial issue. The serial issues are placed in a box by year, and will not be sent to the bindery until RFID Data Model for Libraries becomes a standard (see Data Model section of Chapter 2 for more information). At that time, CSU will use the Data Model's Ordinal Part Number for bound periodicals. WNPL also tags each periodical issue; however, the library does not bind any issues.

Once the initial conversion is completed, how should the library process new materials?

We recommend that the library continue to bar code its materials as usual or have bar-code numbers printed on tag overlays or on the tags. Both CSU and WNPL use overlays with preprinted sequential bar-code numbers.

Should a protective label be placed over each RFID tag?

Using protective labels is cost-effective and provides additional protection for the RFID tag while camouflaging its purpose.

How are multipart items tagged?

The library may decide to use only one RFID tag per item, regardless of how many parts that item may include. If it does so, it may tag the case or one of the parts. The best practice is that the last part of a set is tagged since that is the one most likely to be left in the patron's player. If individual item parts are uniquely identified in the library's circulation database, they may be individually tagged and identified with their item identification numbers. Even if the library's circulation database is not set up to uniquely identify the individual item parts, it is still possible to include information in the tag indicating, for example, "part 1 of a 4 part set." Doing so secures each part independently and informs the library or patron whether all parts of a multipart set are present at the time of check out and check in if the system is configured to look for multipart sets. The reading of multipart sets consisting of CDs or DVDs is subject to the overall limitations that apply to discs that are tagged with the "donut" style hub tag.

Can collection conversion be done in the stacks?

Yes. During the retrospective conversion process, a mobile programming station can be wheeled through the aisles. It is important during the retrospective conversion that all materials coming into the library, whether they are new or returned, be programmed before being returned to the shelves.

Do vendors' software inform you whether tags are programmed correctly?

Most have a verification process to ensure that all the digits in the bar code are read from the bar-code label and written to the tag. While most software offers the user the ability to visually verify that the number being written to the tag is correct, this extra time-consuming step should not be necessary. Both CSU and WNPL found that the error rate in tag programming was close to zero.

Should libraries lease conversion stations to facilitate the initial conversion process?

This depends, of course, on the time frame available for conversion. Many vendors offer tag programming stations that also dispense the tags. Depending on the volume of new items processed each year by the library, this equipment may not be needed on a permanent basis. Both CSU and WMPL leased conversion kits to expedite the process.

Is there any reason that a tag should be placed on an item but not programmed at the very same time?

No. As noted above, the time required to program a tag is minimal. In addition, not programming a tag at the same time as it is inserted into the item can easily lead to confusion.

Once a tag has been programmed, can it be reprogrammed at a later time?

While some vendors offer an option that allows the bar-code numbers on tags to be reprogrammable, the best practice is to "lock" the bar-code number after it is converted. Other nonmission critical information, such as genre or shelving area information, may be changed at a later time.

A.6   RFID READERS

What is the read range of the passive tags used in libraries?

The read range of readers used in library circulation functions is generally between 6 inches and 12 inches (see Chapter 3 for the difference between WORM and R/W tags). A larger reading range is not necessarily better since it is important that only the tags that are supposed to be read are read. Security pedestals have ranges between 18 inches and 24 inches, creating aisles of 3 feet to 4 feet.

Will RFID hardware interfere with other electronic devices in the library?
RFID hardware will not create any interference with current security systems, PCs, phones, or other electronic devices.

Are there health risks associated with RFID?
No. The Apex RFID system is not harmful to persons, including those with hearing aids or pacemakers.

Is the RFID system in any way harmful to library materials, including audio-visual materials?
No.

Can an RFID-based circulation system work with any type of library card?
Yes. Most libraries continue using bar-coded patron cards after they have transitioned to RFID.

Does the RFID have any effect on magnetic media?
RFID hardware will not affect magnetic media, including library cards, credit cards, videocassettes, and the like.

What prevents reader collision?
Some vendors provide readers that are manufactured with a ferrite coating that prevents reader "bleed," a phenomenon that occurs when tags outside the field are unintentionally detected by the reader. The ferrite coating constrains the field to its specified area. As a result, readers can operate in close proximity to one another without fear of collision.

How much does an RFID reader used at a staff station cost?
Staff-station readers generally run between $2,000 and $4,000, depending on the size and power and whether staff software is bundled into the price.

A.7   STAFF CIRCULATION STATIONS

Is SIP2 or NCIP required for staff circulation stations? Can the library continue to use its ILS circulation screens?
Most vendors require that their own software be used at staff stations interfacing the library's ILS through SIP or NCIP. However, at least one vendor, including CSU's and WNPL's vendor, the Integrated Technology Group (ITG), offers an option of keeping the ILS circulation module open and operative at all time, delivering data derived from RFID tags the same way that data from bar codes is currently delivered.

Can a bar-code scanner and an RFID reader work concurrently?
Yes. Most libraries continue using bar-coded patron cards or magnetic patron cards, and many libraries may choose not to place RFID tags in all items. In most cases, the library needs to be able to process materials that come from other libraries that do not have RFID tags, thereby necessitating a bar-code scanner.

A.8   SELF CHECK-OUT

In what situations would checking out items one at a time be recommended?
The proliferation of self service in retail locations, particularly supermarkets, has helped train customers to check themselves out. To maintain consistency with the retail

processes that are bar-code based, libraries using RFID may choose to have materials processed one at a time. In addition, CDs and DVDs, particularly if tagged with the hub donut style tags, are best processed one at a time.

How many items may be checked out at one time simultaneously?

While the anticollision features of RFID tags and systems usually allow over 20 items to be processed simultaneously, tests have indicated that people start making counting mistakes when they go above five items and certainly over ten. Therefore, stack size should be limited. After one stack is processed, the patron may continue to check out additional stacks up to the total item limit set by the library.

If a stack of items is being processed simultaneously, what happens if an RFID tag is absent from one or more items or if one or more tags are not detected?

Vendors approach this problematic issue in different ways. See the self check-out section in Chapter 3.

A.9   AUTOMATED CHECK-IN

What options are available for automated check in?

Two options are generally available. The library may choose to install an RFID-configured standard style in-wall book drop similar to what they may already be using. Alternatively, the library may opt for a kiosk style return that offers a variety of patron interface options and accept bar-coded materials in addition to RFID-tagged items. In either case, as items pass through the system, they are automatically checked into the library's database. In some systems, the security bits on the tags will also be reactivated at this same time. Some automated returns system may be configured to generate a receipt for the patron. On the staff side of things, as an item on reserve is returned, an audio alarm may be sounded so that staff in the area may immediately pull it for special handling. A report showing all items checked in or items on reserve that have been checked in may be generated. If desired, a separate ticket may be generated for each returned item with a hold status, thereby alerting staff to special and immediate handling needs.

A.10   SORTING

How do automated materials handling (AMH) conveyor-belt sorting systems work?

As items are checked into the ILS, their security bits are reactivated and then items are separated into various bins according to library-defined criteria. In the simplest three-bin system, for example, items would most likely be sorted by holds (this bin would have a receipt printer attached that produces a ticket with information about the patron waiting for that item), by library items to be re-shelved, and by exceptions. Beyond three bins, there is virtually no limit to the number of sorting locations that can be created.

A.11   SECURITY

Is there an option available that will inform the library of items that have passed through the security gates without their security bits being disarmed?

Most vendors offer this option. When the security gates detect an "on" security bit, they will also record the item ID number of that same tag. This information may be uploaded periodically in batch mode to a computer. Alternatively, a computer can be connected permanently to the security system so that staff can see in real time the item number of the tag that has set off the alarm at the security gate. When multiple items are within the reading field, the item identification performance may not match the performance of the security-bit detection.

Does the security system require a separate server?

RFID WORM systems require a separate server. No separate server is required for R/W systems since the security system does not interface with the ILS and, as such, there is no need to connect to it.

Do the security gates need to be located away from metal door frames or computers?

Gates should be at least 2 feet away from metal door frames and 8 feet away from computers.

What design and installation options are available for security gates?

Some vendors offer customized wood covers designed to match the library's décor. In addition, some provide the option of mounting gates into the floor or into portable base plates. The latter option may also eliminate the need to drill into flooring for the purpose of placing conduit.

Can an RFID library use EM security?

Yes, an RFID library can use magnetic strips for security together with RFID tags in items. However, many of the advantages of RFID are lost when taking this approach.

Should RFID technology be implemented for materials' security purposes only?

While the detection and false alarm rates of RFID security gates can be, depending on the system, better than traditional EM technology used in libraries, the tags are more difficult to conceal and the signals easier to block. Dishonorable users may use tin foil to wrap books and pass the security gates without triggering the alarm system. Also, for many libraries, DVDs and CDs are the items most likely to be stolen and these items are the most difficult to secure, using any of the extant technologies. Libraries may want to continue using AV locking cases on their most valuable/most vulnerable items. That said, libraries that intend to eventually implement full RFID functionality may well consider starting out using RFID for security purposes only.

A.12   SHELF READING

What can an RFID shelf reader do?

Shelf wands read items as the wand's antenna is waved along the base of shelves. The most basic function is the simple collection of bar-code numbers for inventory purposes. The system may communicate with the library's database (either uploaded into the reader or through wireless communication) to detect items that have been mis-shelved (see question below). Specific items may be uploaded into the laptop from the database so that, when operating in tag search mode, an alarm will sound when a designated item is detected. In addition to these functions, some systems also activate the security bits on any tags that may be in the off position.

Will the inventory wand tell me if items are in EXACT shelf order?

Generally, no. It can alarm the user when an item is outside a designated range (usually, no less than 6 inches away from its proper location). In practice, this is sufficient so that an individual looking for a book will indeed find it.

There are many questions to which we have no answers, such as:

What if tags could be easily created at home or office by using a device like a printer?

What if every cell phone served as an RFID reader?

How then would RFID be used, and who would benefit?

Would such a development be a gateway to making RFID a disruptive force?

Will the current standards encourage such developments or try to thwart them (Heinrich, 2005, p. 225)?

REFERENCES

American Library Association. (2005). *Guidelines for implementing RFID technologies in libraries: Privacy and intellectual freedom concerns.* Retrieved November 24, 2005, from http://www.ala.org/ala/oif/oifprograms/openhearings/relatedlinksabc/draftrfidguidelines.htm

Heinrich, C. (2005). *RFID and beyond.* Indianapolis, IN: Wiley Publishing. TI RFID Newsletters. (2005, November/December). *Privacy and security.* Retrieved December 17, 2005, from http://www.ti.com/rfid/docs/news/eNews/

Appendix B

Budget Sheet

Initial budget. Initial budget includes tags, labor, circulation workstation, self check machine, automated book drop(s), sorter with a number of bins, inventory scanner(s), security gates, installations, training fees, bar-code scanner(s), bar-code printer(s), shipping, other equipment, purchasing and/or leasing conversion workstations, and maintenance fees for the first year. The CSU's initial budget sheet is shown in Table Appendix B.1.

Table Appendix B.1. Initial budget sheet.

Initial Budget Sheet			
Components	Quantity	Unit Price	Costs
Tags			
Labor: hours			
Conversion Station: purchasing			
Conversion Station: leasing			
Circ Station			
Self check machine			
Book drop			
Sorter with bins			
Inventory scanner			
Security gates			
Installation fees			
Barcode printer			
Barcode scanner			
Other equipment			
Training fees			
First year maintenance fees			
Total			$

Ongoing budget. The price of a tag is about 55 cents in 2006 depending on the volume your library orders. A medium-size library that adds 10,000 new items annually needs $5500 ongoing budget for tags in 2006.

All types of readers and hardware require budget for annual maintenance costs. It could be from 8% to 15% of the RFID hardware costs depending on your negotiation with the vendor. Annual maintenance costs of SIP2 or NCIP software could be from 5% to 10% of the software price.

Appendix C

Conversion Guidelines: A Sample

CHICAGO STATE UNIVERSITY LIBRARY'S RFID CONVERSION GUIDELINES (PRINT MATERIALS)

The process described below is vendor specific and applies only to the Integrated Technology Group (ITG) conversion software. The guidelines can be used as a reference for other vendors' conversion software.

1. If a book is damaged according to your judgment, put it on a book truck labeled "Binding" with a pink sticker. Do not put an RFID tag on a damaged book.
2. Place the label over the tag first, so it becomes a tag with label for quicker handling. Place the tag with label inside the back cover (from bottom up) close to the spine.
3. Alternate the tags as shown in the four positions in Figure Appendix C.1.
4. Turn on the computer, and start the Tagging software.
5. Click the "Write" tag button.
6. Click the cursor into the "Bar Code" entry field.
7. Place the tag in the center of the reader and scan the bar code with the bar-code scanner.
8. When the tag has written, it is normally set to automatically read the tag in the window box in the upper right corner. You should confirm that the tag was programmed correctly by checking the bar-code number for accuracy. Make sure that the security bit status is on, sorting information is correct, and the locked status is set for the tag.
9. If a book does not program successfully, make three more attempts to program it. If it is still unreadable, it should be put into a "Bad Tags" envelope and a good tag should be placed on the book.

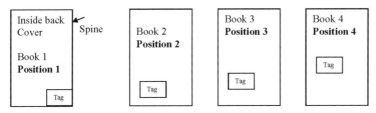

Figure Appendix C.1.   Four tag positions in four different books.

Please pay attention to the following:

- It is very important to keep books in the same order as they are on the shelf.
- Move through the shelves from left to right and from top to bottom in a range.
- Tags marked with "NOK" are defective tags and should be put into the "Bad Tags" envelope.
- If a book has no bar code, put it on a book truck with a blue sticker.
- If a book has other problems, please contact your supervisor or put it on a book truck with a brief note (a purple sticker).
- Write down the last book you programmed on a piece of paper and record it in the RFID TAGGING 3-ring binder.
- Do not place the rolls of blank tags close to the tagging station. Keep the roll you are using about 3 feet away from the reader when the power is on.

Appendix D1

Survey Results of Library RFID Products

Appendix D1. Survey Results of Library RFID Products.

Features/Vendors	3M	Bibliotheca	ITG	Libramation	ST LogiTrack	Tech Logic
Tag memory/EAS bit frequency	2048 bits	Chips of 512 bits to 2 kilobits are used / 13.56 MHz	The Apex RFID system is designed for use with either Tagsys 370 or Folio 320 tags. Both are read/write tags operating at 13.56 MHz. The Folio 320 has a 256 bit memory organized into four data blocks, each of which can be independently locked. The 370 has a kilobit memory. The 320 has a unique Tagsys tag feature that uses a dedicated EAS (Electronic Article Surveillance) burst at 106 kHz. The 370 EAS bit communicates at 13.56 MHz.	1024 bits/13.56 MHz		869 user bits/13.56 MHz

Appendix D1. Continued.

Features/Vendors	3M	Bibliotheca	ITG	Libramation	ST LogiTrack	Tech Logic
AV tag memory/EAS bit frequency	Chips of 512 bits to 2 kilobits are used/13.56 MHz		Same as above	1024 bits/13.56 MHz		869 user bits/13.56 MHz
Tag physical size	48 mm × 57 mm		2" × 2"	86 × 54 mm	50 × 50 mm	45 × 45 mm (1.7" × 1.7")
AV tag physical size			The CD/DVD "donut" tag is approximately 1.56" in diameter.	CD = 38 mm/ VHS = 128 × 19	Diameter 40 mm	40 mm (1.56") diameter
ISO 18000-3 compliant tag or propriatory tag	ISO 18000-3 Mode 1	ISO 18000-3 compliant	The 370 tag utilizes a Phillips manufactured chip and is ISO 15693 compliant, making it compliant with ISO 18000 but without the fast reading features. Better functionality is achieved with the Tagsys Folio 320, an ISO 18000-3 compliant tag.	ISO 18000-3 compliant	ISO 18000-3 compliant	ISO 18000-3 compliant tag (ISO 15693 available)
Do you have "self monitoring software" that checks and repairs the self checkout machines?	No	Remote administration possible	Apex XpressCheck™ can be monitored remotely and messages can be sent to staff stations automatically when a patron experiences a block of any sort. The machines can also be accessed remotely for diagnostic purposes. There is no utility at present that automatically alerts staff when there is a problem with the machine.	Yes, Diagnostics	No	The software has some diagnostics that offer possible solutions to connectivity problems.

144

Do you have build in backward compatibility in all types of readers?	Yes	All readers supplied today for use with the tag currently used, the 370, are compatible with the earlier generation of tags, the Folio 220.	Yes	Yes	Yes except a certain reader is necessary for our legacy clients currently using non-ISO tags.
Do you have build in backward compatibility in the security gates?		Yes. Gates will detect all Tagsys manufactured tags.	Yes. Read all ISO tags		Yes except a certain gate is necessary for clients currently our legacy using non-ISO tags.
Do you have antennas automatic tuning feature in the gates?	Optional	There are no automatic tuning features in gates. However, unlike electromagnetic security gates, once tuned, they do not require retuning.	Yes		Yes
EAS security burst frequency/features	AFI is used for compatibility resons with ISO standards.	The 320 has a unique Tagsys tag feature that uses a dedicated EAS burst at 106 kHz. The 370 EAS bit communicates at 13.56 MHz.			Any tag that incorporates a Phillips chip has EAS capabilities, and all Phillips chip tags have the same features. As new features are introduced, we incorporate the functionality in our systems.

Appendix D1. Continued.

Features/Vendors	3M	Bibliotheca	ITG	Libramation	ST LogiTrack	Tech Logic
Promotion or incentive programs	Please call	Exhibitions, Biblio Bus Tour	Vernon Library Supplies, Inc., Technology Rewards Program puts 20 cents of every dollar you spend on its products towards the purchase systems and support services from ITG (program effective 8/1/02).	Multiple unit discounts		Special pricing is available for volume orders.
Experience with Automated Retrieving System (using RFID for remote storage site retrieving)			While ITG is installing its Apex RFID system at Chicago State University, which at the same time is implementing an ARS system, it is not clear at this time that there is a special link between the two.			We have two products that fit this description: Distribution—Items are recorded as they are placed in a bin. When the bin arrives at a target location, the bin's number is entered which automatically checks in all the items inside. Patron Reserve—Staff fill this device with reserved items which are automatically dispensed when patrons present their patron cards at a book drop.

Total number of RFID libraries (see list of RFID libraries for detail)	70 + worldwide	20+	15+	70+	70+ individual locations for a total of over 350 check-out and back-room stations (29 library systems)
Partners of ILS	Various	SirsiDynix	SirsiDynix, TLC, III	Partners of ILS: AMLIB by Infovision Pty Ltd. Classic by SIRSI (formerly by DRA) Horizon by Dynix Pty Ltd. Kolas (Korean) Millennium by Innopac Q-Series Total by Transtech Unicorn by SIRSI VISTA by Carl Corporation VLIB by Vtech System Virtual by VTLS	TLC (Library• Solution, CARL• Solution), SirsiDynix (Horizon, Dynix ILS, Unicorn, DRA), III (Millinnium), Polaris, Sagebrush (Infocentre)
ILS of current customers	Various	Sirsi/Dynix, Endearor	SirsiDynix, TLC, III		All the above products except Sagebrush, i.e., TLC, SirsiDynix, III, Polaris

Appendix D1. Continued.

Features/Vendors	3M	Bibliotheca	ITG	Libramation	ST LogiTrack	Tech Logic
Manufacturer	Texas Instrument	Various	ITG uses tags and readers manufactured by Tagsys. Apex XpressCheck™ is manufactured by ITG using Tagsys RFID hardware, standard computer components, and cabinetry made specifically for ITG. Sorting solutions are manufactured by FKI Logistex according to ITG design.		ST LogiTrack	Tech Logic, Feig and Tagsys
Outstanding features of your services		Very good software, full compatibility of all ISO chips, no proprietary system, large installation basis and according experience, special tag for CDs.	Please see separate document.	Have a complete solution.		Software is made to work with the library's existing equipment. Systems are customized to the library's needs. We offer the only sorting system that sorts items to specific areas on a book truck and the only conveyor system that can move items vertically up and down (useful when the book drop is above or below

	the floor with of the sorting system). Circulation work station can be used with Personal Payment System (PPS). (PPS is the hardware necessary to accept any combination of credit cards, bills, and coin to pay fines or fees.)				West of the Mississippi: Mike Thuman 800 644-5813 // East of the Mississippi: Tom Loy 888 999-8629
Contact information	Steve McNabb slmcnabb@mmm.com 800-328-0067 × 3	usa@bibliotheca-rfid.com; emmett.erwin@bibliotheca-rfid.com; rod.whitlow@bibliotheca-rfid.com	Shai Robkin President and CEO Integrated Technology Group Tel. 877-207-3127 × 105 770-446-1128 × 105 Fax. 877-207-3129 shai.robkin@integratedtek.com www.integratedtek.com	Frank Mussche frankm@libramation.com 12527-129 ST Street NW Edmonton, AB T5L 1H7 Canada Voice: 780-443-5822 Ext. 101 Toll Free: 1-888-809-0099 Fax: 780-443-5998 http://www.libramation.com	Yvonne Cheong, yvonnecheong@stlogitrack.com; LogiTrack Pte Ltd, Blk 1003 Bukit Merah Central, Redhill Industrial Estate, #03-10, Singapore 159836; DID: (65) 6 2772 866, Fax: (65) 6 2772 886, HP: (65) 9747 3924, www.stlogitrack.com;

Appendix D2

A Survey Letter

On October 16, 2005, a survey was sent to eight vendors to collect data of their RFID products. The vendors are 3M, Bibliotheca, ChechPoint, ITG, Libramation, ST Logi-Track (in Singapore), Tech Logic, and VTLS, of which six vendors returned the surveys along with pictures of their products. A consent form was sent with the survey to request for vendors' permission to use the survey data and pictures. The authors truly appreciate the efforts from 3M, Bibliotheca, ITG, Libramation, ST LogiTrack (in Sigapore), and Tech Logic. These companies provided important information. With the critical information, librarians could compare the products/services and make better decisions when purchasing RFID products. The following is a sample letter:

October 16, 2005
Emmett Erwin
CEO
Bibliotheca RFID Library Systems
Office 248 358 0376
Fax 248 356 9926
emmett.erwin@bibliotheca-rfid.com

Dear Mr. Erwin:

I am writing a publication on RFID and would appreciate it if you would complete the attached spreadsheets and send the survey back via e-mail by November 14, 2005, along with pictures of the following products.

I also need your permission to reprint pictures and spreadsheet data. Enclosed is a permission form.

If you could fax or mail a signed copy to my office, I would appreciate it very much.

Sincerely,

Pictures needed:
Tag outside
Tag inside
Conversion station
Leased conversion station
Circulation workstation
Self-check stand alone
Self-check desktop
Inventory reader
Inventory reader—inside
Security gates
Security gate—inside
Automated check in with sorting conveyor
Automated check in with sorting conveyor—inside
Outsourcing RFID conversion project
Other pictures

Request for Permission to Reprint

We hereby request permission to reprint material from your survey including spreadsheet data and product pictures. If you do not own copyright to this material, please indicate whom we should contact (e-mail, name, address, city, state, zip code, and telephone number).

These data and pictures are to appear without change in the following (the authors are to synthesize the spreadsheet data):

Work tentatively titled: RFID Handbook for Librarians
Written by: Connie Haley, Lynne Jacobsen, and Shai Robkin
Published by Library unlimited
Projected to be printed in early 2006

We are asking for nonexclusive worldwide permission to use this material in a book we are producing, along with permission for incidental use in promoting the book and the rights to grant permission for the reproduction of any pages on which this material appears.

Approval can be signified by completing the bottom section of this letter and returning the letter to us. Thank you for your consideration.

Appendix E

On Tag Sorting Features

A SAMPLE OF CHICAGO STATE UNIVERSITY LIBRARY'S ON TAG SORTING FEATURES

On tag sorting features described below are vendor specific and apply only to the Integrated Technology Group (ITG) tags and software. The sample profile of the Chicago State University's on tag sorting is shown in Table Appendix E.1. This sample can be used as a reference for librarians when they are profiling an on tag sorting feature. The term ARS stands for automated retrieving system, which is an automated storage and retrieving system.

On Tag Sorting: Document from Vendor

Overview.
Additional information about on tag sorting features may be included in other sections as applicable. Before you begin tagging, you should fill out the sorting questionnaire provided by ITG. If you decide against on tag sorting before you begin tagging, it may be very difficult to implement later.

If you plan to use on tag sorting features, ITG will assist you with the initial configuration details. Understanding this topic may be somewhat confusing until you work with some real-life examples.

If you plan to use on tag sorting, you must first determine the categories to be used before any tags are programmed. Individual items should be assigned to the corresponding category for that item as each tag is programmed. Individual items can be reassigned later to any of the original categories, but it can be time consuming if you are attempting to recategorize large quantities of items. The categories themselves cannot be easily changed at a later time, as doing so may require reassigning/rewriting every tag programmed using the old category scheme. Adding new categories at a later time is possible as long as other, unused "slots" are available in the sorting "tables." But after making any change to any sorting table, you will need to carefully copy the sorting data to all other systems that use on tag sorting.

Table Appendix E.1.   Location information coded on the RFID tag.

	This field is visible to user programming tags and at check-out stations – each field must be UNIQUE	This field is NOT visible to user for programming or at staff stations. Only visible when read at return station
Field#	Sort	Location
0	Other	n/a
1	Gen Coll – Mainstacks	Third&Fourth Floors-Gen Coll
2	Gen Coll – ARS	ARS-Gen Coll
3	New Books	First Floor-New Books
4	Reserves – Circ Desk	Circ Desk-Reserves
12	Black Studies – ARS	ARS-lack Studies
21	Archives – 3NW	Third Floor Northwest-Archives
22	Archives – ARS	ARS-Archives
31	Curr Center – 3SW	Third Floor Southwest-Curriculum Center
32	Curr Center – ARS	ARS-Curriculum Center
41	Gov Pubs – 2NE	Second Floor Northwest–Gov Pubs
42	Gov Pubs – ARS	ARS-Gov Publications
51	Media Coll – 1E	First Floor East-Media Collections
52	Media Coll – ARS	ARS-Media Collections
62	Microforms – ARS	ARS-Microform
71	Music Coll – 3NW	Third Floor Northwest-Music Collections
72	Music Coll – ARS	ARS-Music Collections
81	Periodicals – 2SE	Second Floor Southeast-Periodicals
82	Periodicals – ARS	ARS-Periodicals
91	Reference – 2NW	Second Floor Northwest-Reference
92	Reference – ARS	ARS-Reference
93	Reference – Rdy Ref	Ready Reference
101	Special Coll –3NW	Third Floor Northwest-Special Coll
102	Special Coll – ARS	ARS-Special Coll

Programming tags with on tag sorting can take a little longer per item than tagging without on tag sorting, and may require a little more attention to detail for the people programming the tags. When using the on tag sorting feature, the sorting information is represented as a simple number stored on the tag itself. When the tag is read, the sorting information is determined by reading the number stored on the tag and comparing it to the categories listed in the sorting table referenced in the application "ini" file. For example, an RFID tag may simply have a number "3" in the part of the tag specific to sorting. However, when the application reads a 3 as the sorting number on the tag, the application calls to the entry table in the ini file and finds that category 3 is listed as "Juvenile Fiction." These text-based tables must reside in the appropriate ini file for each application that may use on tag sorting features. Care must be taken to make sure the exact copy of each table is copied and pasted correctly into the correct ini file for each copy of each application that will use on tag sorting in the library or library system. Similarly, if you later make a change to the sorting table for one application, you must usually correctly copy this table into each ini file for all other installations of the applications that use on tag sorting. This process is not extremely difficult or time consuming, but does require attention to detail and thoroughness.

Please contact your warranty support provider for a walk-through and assistance with any procedure involving setting up or subsequent changes to the sorting table for any application.

Tag sorting methods.

There are two on tag sorting methods currently available:

Method 1. Allows two sorting fields of up to 16 categories for each field, that is, up to 16 branches (Branch 1, Branch 2, etc.) and up to 16 shelving categories (Fiction, Children's, etc.).

Method 2. Allows a single sorting field of up to 256 categories—branch/shelving categories (i.e., Branch 1 Fiction, Branch 1 Children's, Branch 2 Fiction, Branch 2 Children's, etc.).

With either method, separate tables store the sorting information, allowing easy sorting onto the appropriate book truck. When writing tags, the "sort category" tables are of no consequence. But when you begin using the on tag sorting features in other applications, these tables become important as they simplify sorting. The entries in these sort tables must match by number the corresponding entries in the "Location" tables. So if you have created a shelving category (in table Loc2) called "NonFiction," you should associate a sort entry (in table Sort2) called "Book Truck 1 : Shelf 1" for instance. It is important that the entries in the Location and Sort tables match by number. So in this example, if my NonFiction shelving category in table Loc2 was in the first position (1=NonFiction), then my corresponding sorting text in table Sort2 should also be in the first position (1=Book Truck 1 Shelf 1). After configuring your applications with consistent tables in this manner, a staff member receiving returned items using an Apex reader, for instance, would instantly see on screen the following when checking in a book assigned to this category: Book Truck 1: Shelf 1 and also optionally NonFiction could be displayed. In this way, a staff member using Apex reader or the Manual Sorting features of an Apex tag can easily know the correct book truck and shelving location while simultaneously turning the security bit back on (and with an Apex reader simultaneously checking the item back into your circulation system).

With method 1 sorting (16 branches, 16 shelving categories), it is important to remember that the branch category (Loc1) in the ini files must be consistent among all branches since branch names remain consistent for all branches. While this is true, the shelving categories (Loc2) can differ among branches (i.e., Loc2 may reference "Juvenile Fiction" for Branch1 sorting, but may reference "Children's" at Branch2, etc.). For simplicity (and consistency) we recommend that all branch names and shelving categories remain consistent among branches.

With method 1 sorting, each branch must select from a separate section of the ini file a "this branch" designation, which functions as a filter. If the item is later being read with the Apex reader (Staff Station) or "Manual Assisted Sorting" applications, then the sort location displayed will be based on the branch if the item is from a different branch. The sort location will be based on the "Shelving Categories" if the item was found to be from this branch. So the this branch selection enables the software to determine which of the 2 Location tables to use (Loc1 for branch if the item is from another branch and Loc2 for shelving category if the item is from this branch).

With method 2 sorting, all Locations are assigned in the single table "Loc3" in the appropriate ini file, and the table is copied to the appropriate section in all other applicable ini files for all other applications. There must be consistency among all applications in all branches for the table Loc3 when using sort method 2.

With method 2 sorting, you can combine branch and shelving category information into numerous single entries if desired. For instance, you might have 10 branches and 23 shelving categories. In this scenario you can set up 230 entries in the table Loc3 to contain branch/shelving combinations (example: 1=Branch1 NonFiction, 2=Branch1 Fiction, 3=Branch1 Juvenile, . . . , 100=North NonFiction, 101=North Fiction, 102=North Juvenile, etc.).

With method 2 sorting you may instead decide to have numerous shelving categories and rely on your circulation system or branch info on the spine label for branch information. Alternately, method 2 may need to be followed for branch sorting if a large number of branches need to be referenced. In this scenario, you might continue to use call numbers or other information on the call tag or other book labels to help determine the shelving category.

Appendix F

RFID Resources

F.1 LIBRARY RFID TECHNOLOGY

Library RFID ALA guidelines, American Library Association. *Guidelines for implementing RFID technologies in libraries: Privacy and intellectual freedom concerns.* http://www.ala .org/ala/oif/oifprograms/openhearings/relatedlinksabc/draftrfidguidelines.htm
Library RFID blog http://www.libraryrfid.net/wordpress/
Library RFID data model http://www.bs.dk/standards/rfid/
Library RFID listserv RFID_LIB@listproc.sjsu.edu
Library RFID manufacturer & vendor, CheckPoint http://www.checkpoint.com/
Library RFID manufacturer & vendor, ST LogiTrack http://www.stlogitrack.com/
Library RFID manufacturer, TagSys http://www.tagsys.net/
Library RFID manufacturer, Texas Instruments http://www.ti-rfid.com/
Library RFID vendor, 3M http://www.3m.com/
Library RFID vendor, Bibliotheca http://www.bibliotheca-rfid.com/
Library RFID vendor, Integrated Technologies Group http://www.integratedtek.com/
Library RFID vendor, Libramation http://www.libramation.com/
Library RFID vendor, Tech Logic http://www.tech-logic.com/
Library RFID vendor, Vernon Library Supplies http://www.vernlib.com/
Library RFID vendor, VTLS http://www.vtls.com/
Ringgold OpenRFP http://ww.riverside.lib.ca.us/riverside

F.2 RFID TECHNOLOGY

RFID consulting, IBM http://www.ibm.com/solutions/rfid
RFID consulting, RFID Exchange. There are many white papers on the basics of RFID http:// www.rfidexchange.com/
RFID conference, RFID Journal LIVE. Sponsors RFID Journal annual industry conference, and seminars http://www.rfidjournallive.com/
RFID directory, consulting http://www.rfidintegration.net/rfiddir/
RFID discussion and news http://www.rfidtalk.com/
RFID equipment and tag http://www.affordablerfid.com/

RFID equipment and tag http://www.accusort.com/products/rfid/

RFID guide, Online Guide to RFID Technology Products http://www.rfid-101.com/

RFID information http://www.morerfid.com/

RFID information, Web log, and articles http://rfidtimes.blogspot.com/

RFID information, RFID Collaboration Forum http://www.rfidtribe.com/

RFID Journal, news and articles covering RFID technology. There is a lot of useful information about the RFID industry. This is an advertising driven site. http://www.rfidjournal.com/

F.3   RFID MANUFACTURERS

RFID manufacturer, ACCU Sort Systems, Inc. http://www.accusort.com/

RFID manufacturer, Alien Technology Corporation http://www.alientechnology.com/

RFID manufacturer, Applied Wireless Identification http://www.awid.com/

RFID manufacturer, Fox IV Technologies http://www.foxiv.com/

RFID manufacturer, Intermec Technologies http://www.intermec.com/eprise/main/Intermec/ Content/Technology/RFID/RFID

RFID manufacturer, Markem Corporation http://www.markem.com/

RFID manufacturer, Philips http://www.semiconductors.philips.com/

RFID manufacturer, SAMSys Technologies http://www.samsys.com/ (Acquired by Sirit Inc. on April 13, 2006.)

RFID manufacturer, Sirit Inc. http://www.sirit.com/samsys/

RFID manufacturer, Symbol Technologies, Inc. http://www.symbol.com/

F.4   RFID NEWS

RFID blog http://www.rfid-weblog.com/

RFID news of RFID industry, RFID Gazette http://www.rfidgazette.org/

RFID news of RFID industry http://www.rfidbuzz.com/

RFID news of RFID industry http://www.rfidnews.org/

RFID news of RFID industry http://www.rfidupdate.com/

RFID opposing view http://www.spychips.com/index.html

F.5   RFID ORGANIZATIONS

AIM Global http://www.aimglobal.org/

Federal Communications Commission (FCC), Office of Engineering and Technology, Radio Frequency Safety http://www.fcc.gov/oet/rfsafety

International Commission on Non-Ionizing Radiation Protection, Occupational Safety and Health Administration http://www.osha.org/

Privacy rights http://www.privacyrights.org/

RFID standards, ECPglobal http://www.epcglobalinc.org/

RFID standards, ISO http://www.iso.org/

RFID standards, NISO http://www.niso.org/

F.6   OTHER RESOURCES

Bar code standard, Codabar http://www.makebarcode.com/specs/codabar.html

RFID resources, rules and regulations http://wireless.fcc.gov/

RFID resources, Wikipedia, a free encyclopedia. http://en.wikipedia.org/wiki/

RFID world events, source for information, education, and resources to aid in your understanding of RFID technology and solutions. http://www.rfid-world.com/

Appendix G

Using OpenRFP for RFID Vendor Selection

OpenRFP.

OpenRFP (OpenRFP's e-Procurement services debuts in California; RFID purchase selection aided by Web-based processing, 2006, June 23) is a procurement process that involved the online selection of the functionality requirements for RFID, or any products by libraries. Vendors respond online at the OpenRFP Web site or by using spreadsheets. The new OpenRFP process provides libraries with more control over the comparison of results as each online functional requirement can be weighted individually and scored overall and according to its respective module. The vendor status responses to nearly 400 functional statements are also weighted. Vendors benefit as they can share the response among staff electronically, as well as be able to file their responses right up to the last minute. Paper copies are eliminated except for optional printing of results.

RFID vendor selection.

Riverside County Libraries, CA (www.riverside.lib.ca.us/riverside), uses Ringgold's OpenRFP e-procurement services for its RFP for RFID equipment and services. Seven RFID vendors responded to the online release of the RFP.

Ringgold Inc.

Ringgold's OpenRFP Web services (www.openrfp.com) enables libraries to discover of new products. OpenRFP provides a learning environment where librarians can identify and clarify their needs, translating them to procurement documents or, making directed purchases. The OpenRFP database holds more than 2,200 requirements for online assembly into an RFP or similar document.

Contact.

Ringgold Inc.
www.ringgold.com
Don Chvatal

President
PO Box 368
Beaverton, OR 97075-0368
(503) 977 1313
(503) 977 1314 (fax)
don@ringgold.com

REFERENCE

OpenRFP's e-Procurement services debuts in California; RFID purchase selection aided by web-based processing. (2006, June 23). *Ringgold eMarketing Services*, p. 1.

Suggested Readings

Bhuptani, M., & Moradpour, S. (2005). *RFID field guide: Deploying Radio Frequency Identification systems.* Upper Saddle River, NJ: Sun Microsystems Press.

Boss, R. W. (2003). RFID technology for libraries. *Library Technology Reports, 39* (6), 1–64.

Dawes, T. A. (2004). Is RFID right for your library? *Journal of Access Services, 2* (4), 7–13.

Erwin, E., & Kern, C. (2005). Radio Frequency Identification in Libraries. *Australasian Public Libraries and Information Services, 18,* 20–28. Retrieved September 3, 2005, from http://web6.infotrac.galegroup.com

Kharif, O. (2005, August 11). RFID's second wave: As prices fall and systems improve rapidly, manufacturers are finally starting to embrace the electronic tagging technology. *Business Week Online.* Retrieved September 3, 2005, from the InfoTrac OneFile database.

Schachter, D. (2004). How to manage the RFP process. *Information Outlook, 8,* 10–12. Retrieved September 24, 2005, from the Business Company Resource Center database.

12 Challenges in Supplier, Vendor Selection. (2000, November). *Control Engineering, 47,* 32. Retrieved September 24, 2005, from the Business Company Resource Center database.

Index

About the Authors

Connie K. Haley is a system librarian at Chicago State University Library.

Lynne A. Jacobsen is Director of Technical Services at the Warren-Newport Public Library in Gurnee, Illinois.

Shai Robkin is President of the Integrated Technology Group.